CCSLC®
Integrated Science

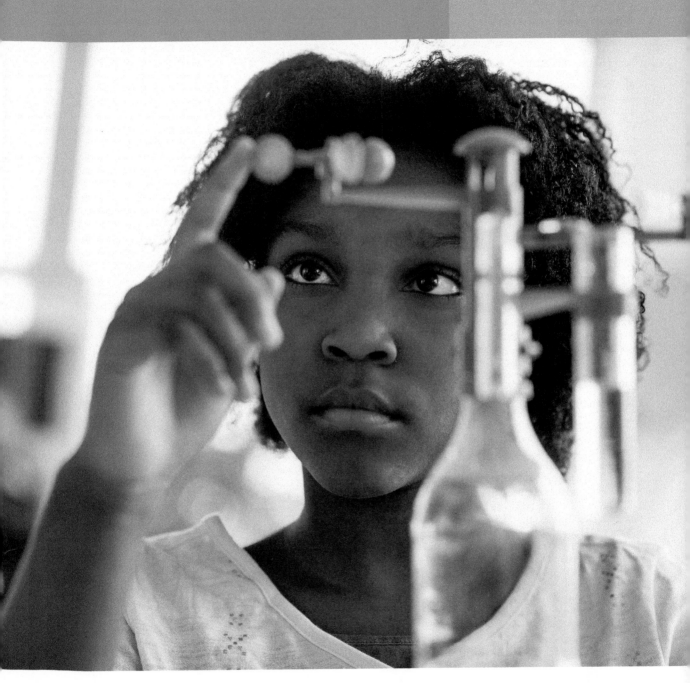

Lawrie Ryan
Pamela Hunte
Victor Joseph

OXFORD
UNIVERSITY PRESS

Great Clarendon Street, Oxford, OX2 6DP, United Kingdom

Oxford University Press is a department of the University of Oxford. It furthers the University's objective of excellence in research, scholarship, and education by publishing worldwide. Oxford is a registered trade mark of Oxford University Press in the UK and in certain other countries

British Library Cataloguing in Publication Data
Data available

978-14-0-857794-3

9 10 8

Paper used in the production of this book is a natural, recyclable product made from wood grown in sustainable forests. The manufacturing process conforms to the environmental regulations of the country of origin.

Printed and bound by CPI Group (UK) Ltd, Croydon, CR0 4YY

Acknowledgements

Cover image: JGI/Tom Grill/gettyimages; p2 Bruce Laurance/gettyimages; p3 SensorSpot/gettyimages; p4 OUP; p4 Mediablitzimages / Alamy Stock Photo; p22 Tibor Bognar/Corbis; p23 Source: http://www.skyscrapercity.com/showthread.php?t=1620611&page=4; p26 PHOTO FUN/Shutterstock; p35 BlackLight Films - Louie Schwartzberg/gettyimages; p35 Kkulikov/Shutterstock; p36 Mark Evans/gettyimages; p37 Sue Robinson/123RF; p37 Gifford & Co / Stockimo / Alamy Stock Photo; p40 Howard Davies / Alamy Stock Photo; p40 Don Johnston / Alamy Stock Photo; p38 www.BillionPhotos.com/Shutterstock; p44 SCIENCE PHOTO LIBRARY; p44 SCIENCE PHOTO LIBRARY; p54 John de la Bastide/Shutterstock; p58 Jason Edwards/gettyimages; p68 kevin walsh / Alamy Stock Photo; p70 Vicki Wagner / Alamy Stock Photo; p71 Cathy Melloan / Alamy Stock Photo; p84 Mediscan/Corbis; p84 OUP; p84 OUP; p88 VOISIN/PHANIE/phanie/Phanie Sarl/Corbis; p89 Jens Molin/Shutterstock; p89 kozmoat98/gettyimages; p89 ThomasLENNE/Shutterstock; p92 PCN/Corbis; p95 Eye Ubiquitous/REX Shutterstock; p96 William James Warren/gettyimages; p97 Robert Harding Picture Library Ltd / Alamy Stock Photo; p100 amornchaijj/Shutterstock; p101 Robert Harding Picture Library Ltd / Alamy Stock Photo; p104 Comstock Images/gettyimages; p109 Ryan Pike/123RF; p112 Antenna/gettyimages; p113 HECTOR RETAMAL/gettyimages; p116 Science & Society/gettyimages; p120 Richard Gardner/REX Shutterstock; p122 SCIENCE SOURCE/gettyimages; p122 Zephyr/Science Photo Library/Corbis; p124 Craig Holmes / Alamy Stock Photo; p125 Julian Finney - FIFA/gettyimages; p126 Flint/Corbis; p143 Monkey Business Images/Shutterstock; p144 Hybrid Images/cultura/Corbis; p144 Vragovic, Will/ZUMA Press/Corbis; p146 claudiodivizia/123RF; p148 Andrea Izzotti/123RF; p150 Sawaya Photography/gettyimages; p153 OUP; p155 AFP/gettyimages; p156 Mohamed Osama/123RF; p157 AFP/gettyimages; p158 Catherine Karnow/Corbis; p159 Emmanuel Joly/gettyimages; p162 1000 Words/Shutterstock; p162 Robert Smith / Alamy Stock Photo; p166 opal1/123RF; p170 CHEN WS/Shutterstock.

Artwork by OKS Group and OUP.

Contents

Contents

*This topic is not part of the CCSLC syllabus.

Introduction

This textbook has been developed exclusively with the Caribbean Examinations Council (CXC®) to be used as a resource by candidates and teachers following the Caribbean Certificate of Secondary Level Competence (CCSLC®) programme. Taking an activity-based approach, the textbook addresses the core skills and content of specific modules of the programme and is designed to lead the students through topics in a way that will enable them to build on previously learnt competencies.

The main purpose of the CCSLC® programme is to prepare individuals to participate fully as productive members of society. It was developed in response to the demand of CARICOM and regional governments for a curriculum that would allow learners with their varied abilities to achieve a sound secondary foundation for further education and training, and facilitate entry into the world of work. Designed to certify the knowledge, generic competencies, attitudes and values that all secondary students should have attained at the end of secondary schooling, the CCSLC® programme sets the standard that regional governments expect from a secondary school graduate. It also provides portable certification that is recognised regionally and internationally.

The programme is competency-based and comprises a core of subjects – English, Mathematics, Integrated Science, Social Studies and Modern Languages (French, Spanish or Portuguese). Generic competencies are targeted for development across the core. These are:

- problem solving
- critical thinking
- informed decision-making
- managing emotions
- developing positive self-concept
- working in groups
- handling conflict
- dealing with adversity and change
- independent learning strategies
- computer literacy
- and technological literacy.

Subject-specific competencies are also targeted for development. These are: oral and written communication, mathematical literacy, scientific literacy, social and citizenship skills, and the ability to function in a foreign language.

The structure and activities of the CCSLC® curriculum are designed to aid in building the attributes that are embodied in the programme's philosophy, and represent the integration of knowledge, competencies and effective qualities critical to the dynamics of lifelong learning, global competitiveness and sustainable development in the region. Mastery of the programme is attained at the student's pace by means of generic summative assessments and an examination.

The textbook is accompanied by a CD that provides additional preparation for the examination in the form of multiple-choice questions. A copy of the PDF can be saved on a PC if students wish to keep their answers for future reference or complete each module test separately.

The answers to the summary questions on each spread, as well as those to the end of module questions can be found online on the Series page at www.oxfordsecondary.com/CCSLC.

Science and technology

Activity

Thinking about science

1 Work in a small group. On a large piece of paper write any words that come to mind when you think of the word 'science'. Record all your suggestions – there are no right or wrong answers.

2 After two minutes, look at your list of words. Work together and try to describe in one or two sentences what science means to you.

3 Now turn your piece of paper over. Note any words you think of when you hear the word 'scientist'.

4 After two minutes, look through your list of words. Now write one sentence describing what your group thinks scientists do.

5 Compare your ideas about 'science' and 'scientist' with those of another group. Try to combine both groups' ideas into one agreed summary to share with the rest of the class.

6 Conduct research using the internet to find out if there are any new ideas.

Science is a way of finding out about the natural world, including how materials and living things behave. It covers a wide variety of areas of study such as:

● biology
● chemistry
● physics
● geology
● astronomy.

Our modern, technological society has developed because of scientists' work in understanding the natural world. Technology can be thought of as the 'application of science'. Technologists provide society with solutions to problems in everyday life, using the ideas developed by scientists. So science provides the 'tools' that technologists use in their work.

Figure 1.1a Technology is the application of science

Activity

How things work

Investigate an everyday technological device. Examples are: a torch, a cellphone, a ballpoint pen, a motor vehicle or a calculator. Then decide:

- why the device was developed
- how it was developed.

Present your findings to the rest of the class. You could use a presentation, an advertisement for TV or radio, or a poster.

Figure 1.1b Technology helps umpires decide when the light is not bright enough for cricketers to continue playing by measuring the light intensity on a lightmeter

Words explained

For the words shown in purple, you can find a definition in the glossary at the back of the book.

Application of scientific knowledge ⟶ Technological advances

Scientists have many different ways to find the answers to scientific questions. These include:

- observing and exploring the natural world
- researching by using secondary sources of information
- fair testing by controlling variables in practical tests
- seeking patterns by carrying out surveys and finding links (correlations)
- using models to explain findings
- identifying and classifying materials, objects and living things
- using and evaluating a technique or design when solving a problem.

When finding the answers to scientific questions, scientists need to develop a wide range of skills, such as:

- forming scientific ideas (these ideas, which are used to explain things, are called hypotheses)
- planning
- observing and measuring
- recording data
- analysing and interpreting data
- evaluating
- working in a team
- communicating findings to other scientists.

Key points

- Science covers a wide variety of areas such as biology, chemistry, physics, geology and astronomy.
- Technology is the useful application of science to benefit society.
- Scientists work together to advance understanding of the natural world, enabling technologists to apply their ideas when solving problems.

Summary questions

1 Explain the difference between science and technology.

2 State five skills that scientists need for their work and why each of these skills is useful.

1.2 Safety first

Safety in everyday life

We come across safety rules and hazard warnings in many aspects of everyday life. Road safety is a good example. Each territory in the Carribean sets out the rules that drivers should follow. This includes road signs that warn of possible danger and inform you of rules, such as speed limits and parking restrictions.

Figure 1.2a Road signs help to keep our roads safe

At home we have products that have hazard signs to warn us about harmful, irritant and corrosive substances. Corrosive substances break down materials by slow chemical reactions.

In science laboratories a variety of hazard symbols are used to warn about potential dangers. You need to know the following symbols in order to work and plan investigations safely in science:

Figure 1.2b Oven cleaner contains strong alkali which is corrosive

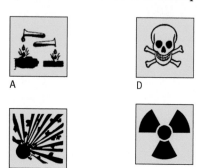

Figure 1.2c Common hazard symbols you need to know. These warn us when we use substances that are corrosive, explosive, harmful or irritant, toxic (poisonous), radioactive or flammable.

Safety in the science laboratory

We also need to behave sensibly in a science laboratory to keep ourselves and those around us safe. Here is a list of some typical laboratory rules:

YOU MUST NOT:

- enter the laboratory unless a teacher is present
- run in the laboratory
- touch any chemicals
- leave experiments unattended
- smell gases directly – fan a little of the gas towards the nose instead
- point the mouth of a test tube towards anyone when heating
- eat or drink in the laboratory
- put solids in the sink.

YOU SHOULD ALWAYS:

- follow the instructions given
- wear eye protection whenever necessary
- read the label on any bottles carefully to make sure it contains the correct chemical and to note any hazard symbols
- report any accidents or breakages to your teacher. If any chemicals get onto your skin or clothing, wash the affected area with a large amount of water and then report it to your teacher
- leave Bunsen burners with a luminous (yellow) flame when not in use (or turn it off)
- tie up long hair
- wash your hands after experiments.

Key points

- Safety symbols are important in all aspects of life.
- In science you need to follow laboratory safety rules and know the common hazard symbols.

Summary questions

1 Draw an example of an unsafe practice in a school laboratory. Then draw the same task again but done safely.

2 Which of the laboratory rules above are designed to protect you against:

   a toxic substances?

   b burns from caustic (acids or alkalis) liquids?

   c burns from naked flames?

3 Which of the hazard symbols, A to F, shown on page 4 warn you of:

   a radioactive substances?

   b substances that can cause skin irritation?

1.3 How scientists work

Exam Tip

The scientific method can be applied in everyday life, not just in a science lab!

The scientific method

The 'scientific method' describes the steps that a scientist goes through in order to investigate a question. It can be summarised by the steps below:

1 **Identify** a problem
2 **Develop** a hypothesis
3 **Plan** an investigation, controlling variables (things that can be changed or varied)
4 **Carry out** experiments, observing and measuring
5 **Record** and process results
6 **Draw conclusions** from the results
7 **Evaluate**, redesigning the method if necessary
8 **Communicate** results and findings

Please note that Scientific method is not a linear process but may require the experimenter to loop back and make changes or adjustments throughout.

In scientific investigations you will have a chance to plan how to answer a question yourself. You design your own method, making sure any tests you plan are safe and fair.

In fair tests you change only the thing (variable) under investigation and keep everything else (all the other variables) the same. Then you know that any changes in your observations or measurements were caused by whatever you chose to change.

In the final stages of an investigation you draw your conclusions, suggest how you could improve your method and share your findings with others.

Planning a whole investigation can be difficult so it is a good idea to use:

● an investigation planner to remind you of the questions you should be thinking about

● a planning grid to help you deal with the variables involved in a fair test (see page 8).

Investigation planner

You can use these questions to help you plan your investigations.

1 What am I trying to find out?
2 a What do I think (predict) will happen?
  b Why do I think this will happen?

Activity

Planning an investigation

Now try planning one of the following investigations.

Ripening fruit

Does green fruit wrapped in newspaper ripen faster than unwrapped green fruit?

Drying objects

Do objects painted black dry faster than objects painted white?

Iron rusting

Do iron objects close to the sea rust faster than those inland?

You will be assessed on 'Planning and designing'.

3 What am I going to change each time? This is your **independent variable**.

4 What am I going to judge or measure each time? This is your **dependent variable**.

5 What will I keep the same each time to make it a fair test? These are your **control variables**.

6 a How will I carry out my tests?

   b How many values for my independent variable will I choose to test?

7 a Is my plan safe?

   b Could anything go wrong and somebody get hurt? (Check with your teacher.)

8 What equipment will I need?

9 a How many readings will I need to take?

   b Do I need to repeat tests?

10 What is the best way to show my results? A table … or a bar chart … or a line graph?

Key points

- Following the scientific method involves; identifying a problem, developing a hypothesis, planning an investigation, carrying out experiments, recording/processing results, drawing conclusions, evaluating and communicating your results and findings.

- The key variables in an investigation are the independent variable and the dependent variable. All other relevant variables should be kept constant in a fair test – these are called controlled variables.

Summary questions

Look at your plan from the last activity above.

1 Identify the independent variable.

2 Identify the dependent variable.

3 List some of the control variables you planned to keep constant.

1.4 Carrying out project work

Collecting evidence

As you know, scientific enquiries are all about finding the answers to scientific questions. Here are some of the approaches you can use:

- observing and exploring
- researching – using secondary sources
- classifying and identifying
- fair testing – controlling variables
- pattern seeking – surveys and correlation
- using models
- using and evaluating a technique or design.

We often call an extended enquiry 'a project'.

In science, we collect evidence to answer the question we are investigating. How we gather the evidence will depend on the question. In a project, it may well involve more than one of the ways listed above. So project work will take several lessons and/or homeworks to complete.

Fair testing

The investigation planner below helps you to plan fair tests:

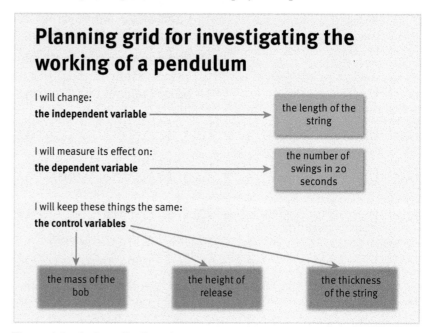

Figure 1.4a An investigation planner

Group work

You might also be working as part of a group in project work.

When you start on a project you must be clear about the question you are investigating. As a group you should discuss this together and sort out the different aspects of the problem. Then you can divide the work up between the members of the group.

Presenting your findings

It is a good idea to try to draw out a plan for the project at this stage. Perhaps use a flow chart.

Try to have a clear idea of what the finished project will look like. Ask yourselves 'What is the best way to share our findings with other people in the class or school?'

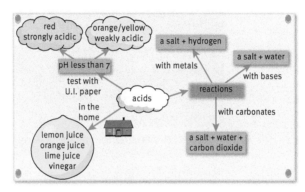

Figure 1.4b There are a variety of ways to present your findings to other people. Posters are just one of them. Can you think of others?

Carrying out research

After your plan, many projects will involve research to find out what other people have found out already.

Before you start any research write down what you know already. Then record what you want to find out.

Decide where to look for the information. Will you use books, videos, CD-ROMs or the internet?

Once you have found some useful information, summarise it in your own words; do not copy or cut-and-paste directly. Also quote the source of your information. Think about whether you can trust it or not.

Summary questions

1 Think about the project you have enjoyed most in your time at school. What was the project and what made it so enjoyable?

2 Write a checklist for a group to evaluate their project when it is finished.

1.5 Communicating like a scientist

When scientists have carried out an investigation, they publish their work for other scientists to discuss. As a young scientist, you should do the same thing. Here is a report written by a student. Some comments on the investigation have been inserted in the boxes.

Figure 1.5a What factors affect how quickly the clothes will dry?

Example of writing up a report of an investigation

Aim

To find out how temperature affects the rate at which water evaporates.

> **Comment**
>
> Another good way to start an investigation is with a clear question. In this case it could be 'How does temperature (*the independent variable*) affect the rate at which water evaporates (*the dependent variable*)?

Hypothesis

The higher the temperature the greater the loss in mass of water from a paper towel in a given time.

> **Comment**
>
> This idea should be explained (that is, give at least one reason) to make a better hypothesis. As it stands this is just a prediction – explain your prediction to write a hypothesis to test.

Plan

Wet paper towels will *be* used *to see* how quickly they dry at different temperatures.

Only the temperature will *be* changed in each test. The paper towels can each *be* wet with 10 cm³ of water (measured in a measuring cylinder). They will *be* put on a Petri dish and then *be* left in different places – on a windowsill in the sun, in a fridge, in a shady room, and outside in a sheltered place.

The temperature at each place will *be* measured with a thermometer and recorded in the table under 'Results'.

The mass of water lost every 10 minutes for half an hour will *be* measured *to see* how quickly the water evaporates. An electric balance or scale will *be* needed to weigh the dry paper towels to make sure they all have the same mass to start with. Then they will *be* reweighed when they first have water added to them on a Petri dish. They will then *be* weighed again at 10-minute intervals once left in the different places.

There are no safety hazards involved in this investigations as long as normal laboratory rules are followed.

Variables

1. The independent variable – We are investigating the effect of changing the temperature. So temperature is our independent variable. This will be the only thing that should change in each test area.

2. The dependent variable – The loss in mass of the paper towel is our dependent variable. (This is used to judge the effect of changing the independent variable – the temperature in this investigation)

3. Control variables – These are all the other variables that might affect the rate of evaporation and should be controlled. They must be kept constant in each test at the different temperatures. These are the control variables:
   - Type of paper towel (so the mass, size, and material used to make the paper towels should be the same)
   - Volume of water soaked into each paper towel to start with,
   - The surface area of the paper towel exposed to the air.
   - The timings when reading the mass (to make fair comparisons after set periods of time).

Comment

This is a well-designed investigation. If you have time for some 'trial runs', this will help you to decide how many readings you need to take and what measuring equipment you will need. In a more complex investigation, a diagram can also help to show your intended method.

Continued

Here is the rest of the student's account of their investigation 'How does temperature affect the loss in mass of water from a paper towel?'

Apparatus and materials

Four paper towels, four Petri dishes, measuring cylinder (10 cm³), electric balance or scale, thermometer.

Results

Place paper towel is left	Temperature (°C)	Mass of paper towel + dish before (g)	Mass of paper towel + dish after 10 mins (g)	Mass of paper towel + dish after 20 mins (g)	Mass of paper towel + dish after 30 mins (g)
On sunny windowsill					
In a fridge					
In a shady room					
Outside in a sheltered place					

Comment

A graph of 'loss in mass of water' (*the dependent variable on the vertical axis*) against 'temperature' (*the independent variable on the horizontal axis*) would show the pattern of results more clearly than the table alone.

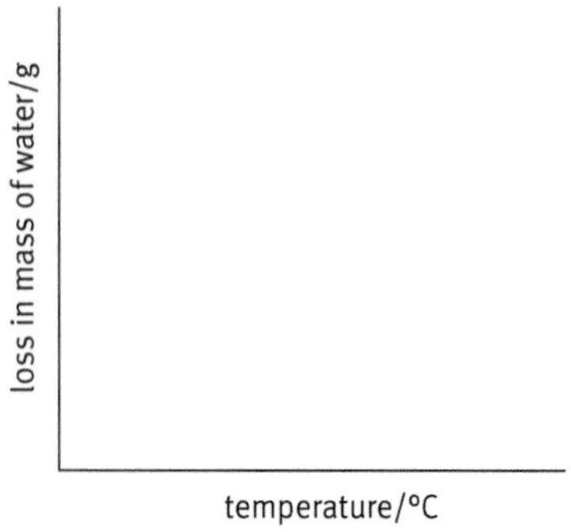

Figure 1.5b Notice that the units are included when we label the axes of a line graph

Discussion (to include conclusion and evaluation)

Conclusion – The warmer it is, the faster the water evaporates.

Evaluation – If I had time I would like to repeat the tests on different days when the temperatures would be different to my original tests on the windowsill and in the shady room.

The temperature might not stay constant in each place I put the paper towels. So it would be better if I took the temperature when I left them, then after an hour and took the average of the two values to plot on a graph.

The electric balance reads to 0.1 of a gram. It would give me more accurate results if the balance gave values to 0.01 of a gram.

Making sure the test is fair (all the control variables are kept constant)

This was quite difficult. When adding 10 cm³ of water to each paper towel we used a small measuring cylinder and reading this accurately was difficult. The error could be + or –0.2 cm³. Using a burette or pipette would make this more accurate.

The paper towels will also have to be crumpled up to fit on the dishes. So it will be difficult to be sure that their surface areas exposed to the air are exactly the same. They could be cut into a smaller shape to fit the dish but then they wouldn't absorb as much water.

Comment

The conclusion is weak here. It does not explain how the data collected support the hypothesis at the start of the report. It should also refer to the particle theory to explain the science involved in evaporation and how it is affected by temperature.

The evaluation is a good discussion of the method used.

Key points

A good way to structure a report of your investigations is to write an aim (or question), hypothesis, plan, apparatus and materials, results (to include table and graph where relevant), and a discussion (to include conclusion and evaluation).

Activity

Carry out and write up an investigation

Write a report of one of your own investigations using the same sections as those used in this topic. It could be a report of one of the investigations on page 7.

OR

Investigate what affects the rate at which a pendulum swings.

You will be assessed on 'Recording and communication', as well as 'Analysis and interpretation'. If you tackle the pendulum investigation you might also be assessed on 'Planning and designing'.

Summary questions

1 Why do scientists use tables to record their results as they carry out investigations?

2 Why do scientists display their data collected on graphs?

3 Look back at Figure 1.5b. Copy the axes of the graph and sketch the line you would expect from the results of an investigation of how temperature affects the loss in mass at the four different locations after a set time.

4 Plot a line graph of the results of an investigation to find out how the length of a spring is affected by the mass suspended from it:

Mass (g)	Length of spring (cm)
0	5.0
50	5.6
100	6.2
150	6.8
200	7.4
250	8.0

5 List three ways in which the student could have improved the investigation described in this topic.

1.6 Publishing results*

When scientists carry out research and make new findings, they need to tell other scientists about their work. In this way, science makes progress. It carries on developing our understanding of the world.

A system called 'peer review' is used before work gets published in scientific journals. A scientist will write a paper and send it to a journal. The journal will organise other scientists to look over (review) the paper before publication. It's a bit like you asking a classmate to check your work before you hand it in.

These reviewers raise any queries with the author of the paper. If they are happy with the author's replies and changes, the paper will be published. Then all scientists can read about the new work. But now and again the system does not stop 'bad science' getting through.

Question 1: Why are scientific papers reviewed before publication?

Case study

In 2001 Dr. Jan Hendrik Schon was a rising star in one of the world's best research establishments. Many important inventions were made there. For example, in 1947 the transistor was developed. Now billions of these are made for our computers every week. Other inventions made there include mobile phones, lasers, communication satellites and internet systems.

Dr. Schon worked in nanotechnology – making incredibly tiny machines. He was trying to make the smallest computer components ever. His team claimed to discover single molecules that could act as transistors.

In just two years he produced 80 publications. However, some scientists started to question some of the data in his publications.

They noticed identical tables of results in different experiments. Even readings that were meant to be random were the same. Other scientists tried out the same experiments themselves. They failed to reproduce Schon's data. So an inquiry took place into Schon's work.

Activity

Great inventions

Carry out some research into the work done since 1925 at the famous Bell Laboratories. Choose one example to write a two minute item for a radio programme about science and technology milestones in the last century.

*This topic is not part of the CCSLC syllabus.

Question 2: Why did scientists start to doubt Schon's work?

The inquiry found that Schon had made up experimental data at least 16 times between 1998 and 2001. They accused him of:

- removing data that disagreed with his predictions and

- making up data from mathematical equations, pretending they were really experimental results.

Schon disagreed with some of their findings. He claimed all his publications were based on experimental observations. However, he did admit making "various mistakes in my scientific work, which I deeply regret." Despite his objections, Bell Laboratories quickly fired Schon.

This has raised questions about the 'peer review' system. The scientists who review the papers might not query the results of work from large institutions or from famous scientists.

Reviewers claim that their job is to check the validity of conclusions drawn from data. They do not to check the data themselves. They trust the scientists to record their actual results. So the system remains open to abuse from dishonest scientists.

To combat this, editors are encouraging reviewers to question any data from single or a small number of experiments – whatever their source!

Key points

- Publishing results allows all scientists to learn about the latest scientific discoveries.

- Peer review is a system meant to ensure that only those investigations that rigorously follow the scientific method are published.

Summary questions

1 Make a list of the discoveries made at the Bell Laboratories.

2 How do scientific journals try to make sure the papers they publish are 'good science'?

3 What kind of things might influence a scientist to publish false data?

4 What do you think can be done to make it harder for 'bad science' to get published? Point out any difficulties your ideas might cause.

5 How do you try to make your own experimental data more reliable?

1.7 Measurement in science

Why measure?

When scientists carry out experiments, they need to report exactly what they have done when publishing their results.

If a scientist adds acid to a metal, other scientists need to know not only the type of acid and which metal, but how much of each was added together. It is not good enough to say 'a little' acid was added or a 'big bit' of metal. This is not precise enough for other scientists to check the results by exactly carrying out the same experiment themselves. That is why scientists use measuring instruments – so they can report, for example, that '12.5 cm^3 of sulphuric acid' was added to '3.4 g of magnesium ribbon'.

Activity

Why we need measuring instruments

Place one hand into a bowl of warm water and the other hand into a bowl of cold water for one minute. Then mix both bowls of water together and place both hands in it and estimate its temperature.

Can you trust your sense of touch to judge temperature? Why not?

Scientists needed a standardised measuring system that all scientists across the world could use. It has been agreed that everyone should use SI units (SI stands for *Système international d'unités*, which in English is the International System of Units). A metre is a metre; no matter where it is measured, it is a standard unit that everyone knows.

Common measurements in science

Length

Length is the distance between two points.

The units for length are the **metre (m), centimetre (cm)** and **millimetre (mm)**.

Scientists use a metre rule to measure length.

Mass

Mass is the amount of matter in an object.

The units for mass are **grams (g)** and **kilograms (kg)**.

Scientists use top-pan balances in the laboratory to measure mass.

Figure 1.7a The top-pan balance shown here reads to 0.1g but more expensive balances will read to 0.01g or 0.001g

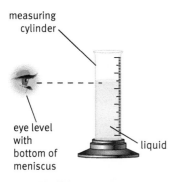

Figure 1.7b When reading the volume get your eye level with the bottom of the meniscus (the curve in the surface of the liquid)

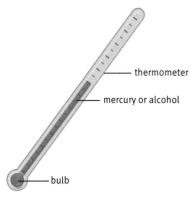

Figure 1.7c A thermometer has a small amount of mercury or alcohol (coloured red) that expands as it gets hotter and rises up a thin tube. Make sure the bulb at the end of the thermometer is within a liquid when measuring the liquid's temperature.

Key points

- Measurements are important in science as we need standardised measures that everyone understands to give accurate and reliable data.
- Length (m), volume (cm³), time (s), mass (g) and temperature (°C) are common quantities measured in science.

Volume

Volume is the amount of space taken up by an object.

The units for volume are **cubic centimetre (cm³)** or **millilitres (ml)** and **cubic metres (m³)**.

Scientists use measuring cylinders of various sizes to measure the volume of liquids.

Time

Time is the measurement of period (how long an event takes place for).

The units for time are **seconds (s)**, **minutes (min)** and **hours (h)**.

Scientists use a variety of timers, such as stop clocks or stopwatches to measure time.

Temperature

Temperature is a measure of the amount of heat energy in a substance.

The unit for temperature is **degrees Celsius (°C)**.

Scientists use thermometers to measure temperature.

All these instruments must be used properly and read carefully to get reliable measurements that can be trusted and that are accurate (giving true values).

Activity

Measuring and recording

Your teacher will give you a chance to measure length, volume, mass, temperature and time. Measure each as accurately as you can. Make sure you select and use the measuring instrument correctly and take care reading the scale.

Record your results in a table. Do not forget to include the correct units.

You will be assessed on 'Manipulation and measurement'.

Summary questions

1 Why is measurement so important in science?
2 Write some instructions for a younger student explaining how to measure:
   a the temperature of water in a beaker
   b the volume of water in a cup.

1.8 Measurements and results

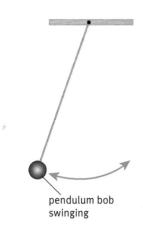

pendulum bob swinging

Figure 1.8a The swinging pendulum investigation

Accuracy

Think about the pendulum investigation again from page 13. What affects the rate at which a pendulum swings.

You might have changed the length of the string in each test and you might have counted the number of swings in 20 seconds.

Whenever you are doing an investigation you should think about how **accurate** the data you plan to collect needs to be.

An accurate measurement is near the true value.

For example, the length of the string measured with great accuracy could be 10.10013 cm. However for your pendulum investigation, a ruler with a millimetre scale will be good enough. It can give the same measurement of length as 10.1 cm (as long as you read it properly).

Recording data

You should also think ahead about how you will record your data. Scientists record data in tables as they carry out their tests.

They usually put the independent variable in the first column. They put the dependent variable in the second column. Any units must be included. So in the pendulum investigation the table would be:

Length of string (cm)	Number of swings in 20 seconds

Some data can be tricky to collect. The data might not be repeatable – if you do the same test again you exactly the same result. You can have more trust in your measurements if the repeats you carry out are all close together. The data can then be described as **precise** if repeat readings show good agreement. If one of the repeat readings is very different to the others, you should ignore it and try the test again.

However, remember that if you are doing something wrong in each test, repeating tests won't give **accurate** data.

We record repeat readings in a table with the second column split up into smaller columns.

For example:

Length of string (cm)	Number of swings in 20 seconds			
	1st test	2nd test	3rd test	Mean (average)

Activity

Making decisions

A group were investigating how the temperature affects the time it takes sugar to dissolve in water. It was difficult to judge exactly when the sugar had completely dissolved in each test. They decided to do their investigation at 20, 30, 40, 50 and 60 °C.

- Design a table that the group could record their results in.

- They asked their teacher for a stop-watch reading to one hundredth of a second to do their timing. Why did the teacher say that the second hand of the clock on the wall was good enough for this investigation?

You add up the three tests and divide the answer by 3 to work out the mean (average).

For example, if a group repeated a test three times under the same conditions and got results of 49, 46, 48 swings so the mean number of swings for that test is:

$(49 + 46 + 48)/3 = 47$ swings

Key points

- Measurements are accurate if they are near the true value.
- We can reduce the error in measurements by repeating them and working out the mean (average).

Summary questions

1 In the pendulum investigation:

  a What measuring instrument will you need for the length of the string?

  b What measuring instrument will you need to time the 20 seconds?

2 a

Figure 1.8b

  Which balance would give the more accurate measurement of mass when used correctly?

  b Which measuring instrument can give the more accurate measurement: a stopclock which measures to the nearest second or a stopwatch reading to the nearest one hundredth of a second?

  c Which measuring instrument in part b is more suitable for our pendulum investigation?

3 What are the readings shown on the following scales?

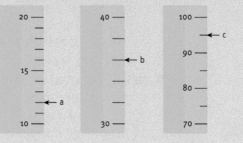

Figure 1.8c

1.9 Caribbean issues and scientists

The Caribbean is one of the most popular places in the world for tourists to visit, with its sunny climate, beautiful sandy beaches, and warm, clear sea. However, there are some issues in the region that can only be solved using science and technology. The important issues are listed below with ways in which scientists are tackling the problems:

Caribbean issues

▶ **loss of agricultural land**
  - ✓ soil conservation methods
  - ✓ terracing
  - ✓ crop rotation

▶ **decrease in potable (drinkable) water sources**
  - ✓ desalination (removing salt from seawater)
  - ✓ recycling waste water
  - ✓ mandatory water tanks for new residential construction

▶ **limited physical resources**
  recycling of:
  - ✓ metals
  - ✓ paper
  - ✓ glass

▶ **costly energy supplies, employing alternative energy sources such as:**
  - ✓ wind farms
  - ✓ biogas
  - ✓ gasohol
  - ✓ solar devices (using the power of sunlight)
  - ✓ hydroelectricity (using water to generate electricity)
  - ✓ natural gas and bagasse

▶ **lower agricultural yields**
  - ✓ hydroponics (growing plants in solutions of nutrients without using soil)
  - ✓ tissue culture (growing plants from bits of plant material in artificial conditions)
  - ✓ greenhouse technology

▶ **increased risk of diseases infecting crops and livestock**
  - ✓ cloning (creating identical copies of living things)
  - ✓ genetically modified organisms (introducing new genes from other living things into an organism)
  - ✓ stem cell research (using young cells that can develop into any type of cell needed)

▶ **risk of physical structures being damaged from weather systems (hurricanes, storms, floods)**
  - ✓ new roof designs
  - ✓ improved building codes.

Activity

Research a Caribbean issue

Choose one of the issues listed above to carry out research on. You can work as part of a small group. Describe the nature of the problem, its cause and what the consequences are if we cannot solve it. Then say how scientists are working to solve the problem and evaluate the progress made so far. Organise your findings into an interesting format that will encourage citizens to read it.

Caribbean scientists

Territory of birth	Name of scientist	Area(s) of work
Trinidad and Tobago	Dr Avril Siung – Chung	oyster production and marine pollution
Guyana	Prof. Nazeer Ahman	social science
Belize	Dr Arleigh Petters	physics/mathematics
	Dr Avery August	cancer research
Jamaica	Dr Thomas P. Lecky	new species of cattle called "Jamaica Hope'
	Dr Errol Morrison	diabetes
Barbados	Dr Oliver Headley	solar energy devices
St. Vincent and the Grenadines	Dr Jeffrey W. Dellimore	behaviour of red blood cells under special conditions
Dominica	Prof. Harrison B. Prosper	high energy physics

Activity

Famous scientists

Choose one of the scientists from the table above to investigate. Alternatively research a different Caribbean scientist of your choice.

In the presentation of your findings include any details of their life before becoming a scientist and any of their other interests. Describe briefly the scientific research they published and what they found out.

Key points

Caribbean scientists are actively involved in research to solve many of the issues that face the region and the rest of the world in the years ahead.

Summary questions

1 Make a table showing five challenges which the Caribbean could face in the years ahead and how science and technology can help solve these issues.

2 In the table above, write the names of the Caribbean scientists who work with living things and state what they are famous for.

1.10 The application of science*

Learning outcomes

At the end of this topic you should be able to:

▸ identify how discoveries are made in science

▸ describe how scientists apply new discoveries to make useful products.

The start of the plastics industry

Have you ever wondered what life would be like without plastics?

Figure 1.9a Lots of everyday articles are made of plastic

A chemist named Leo Baekeland really started our 'plastic society'. Leo was a chemist with a sharp eye for a business opportunity. Although he was born in Belgium in 1863, he made his fortune in America.

He investigated chemicals you could get from coal tar and wood alcohol. Thirty years earlier a German dye chemist had discovered a thick, gooey substance while experimenting. He thought it was just a nuisance. But Leo could see its potential for use as a new varnish.

If Leo heated up the gooey liquid it turned even thicker. And if he did the reaction under pressure it made a hard, translucent solid. He could mould this into any shape he liked. So in 1907 he had made the first synthetic plastic! It had taken him 3 years and thousands of failed experiments. However, his perseverance paid off in the end.

Leo knew how to make the most of his discovery. He patented his new plastic and gave it the trade name 'Bakelite'. He formed a company to make and sell the plastic.

People were quickly using the new plastic, called Bakelite, for everything from buttons to telephones. Leo could make his plastic in a variety of colours. It even became trendy to wear Bakelite jewellery. The plastics revolution had started!

Question 1: How many of the things you have used so far today are made of plastic?

*This topic is not part of the CCSLC syllabus.

Activity

Plastics research

Do some research to find out about either:

a The problems of plastic waste and how we might solve it, or

b The life and work of Wallace Carothers.

Surprising discoveries

In 1938 Dr. Roy Plunkett was experimenting with substances to keep fridges cold. One day he found a waxy solid blocking a gas cylinder. This accidental discovery turned out to be a new **polymer**. A polymer is a very long molecule made by joining lots of smaller molecules. This polymer was called polytetrafluoroethene or PTFE.

It was sold as Teflon®. This special polymer has special 'non-stick' properties. It is also very unreactive. This has led to a wide variety of uses, from non-stick pans to rocket cones.

Question 2: Where might you find PTFE in your kitchen?

In the 1960s the search was on for a new polymer to make lighter-weight tyres. This would help save fuel. Stephanie Kwolek and her team worked on the problem. One day the chemicals she mixed formed a milky liquid, unlike the clear liquid she was expecting. But she didn't just throw the liquid away and start again.

She sent her discovery to the test lab. This stuff was incredible! It was nine times stronger than a similar mass of steel, but was only half the density of fibreglass. Eventually it was marketed in 1971 as Kevlar®. Its strength, low density and heat resistance led to its use in bullet-proof vests, aeroplanes, motorcycle 'leathers' and tennis rackets.

Figure 1.9b Bullet-proof vests are part of the standard police equipment

Key points

Results of scientific investigations often lead to development of new materials that can change how people live.

Summary questions

1 Describe how two creative scientists have helped to change people's lives by their work in the plastics industry.

2 Most plastics nowadays are made from products we get from crude oil – a fossil fuel. How do you think the plastics industry will develop in the next 50 years?

End of module 1 questions

1 Identify the hazard symbols A to F below:

A   B   C   D   E   F

2 As a young scientist, how would you tackle questions a–g? Choose from the types of enquiry labelled i to vii in bold below the questions:

  a How does the angle of a ramp affect the speed of a toy car?

  b What is the temperature on the surface of Jupiter?

  c How can you make your own thermometer?

  d What type of insect is this?

  e Do men have a faster pulse rate than women?

  f Why do metals expand when we heat them up?

  g What happens when calcium metal is added to water?

  i **Observing and exploring the natural world**

  ii **Researching by using secondary sources of information**

  iii **Fair testing by controlling variables in practical tests**

  iv **Pattern seeking by carrying out surveys and finding correlations (links)**

  v **Using models and analogies to explain findings**

  vi **Identifying and classifying materials, objects and living things**

  vii **Using and evaluating a technique or design when solving a problem**

3 Read the following passage about the data you collect in scientific investigations, then answer the questions.

Is your evidence reliable?

If you, or somebody else, were to do the same investigation would you all collect the same data, consistently? If you do, you have collected stronger evidence for any conclusions you reach. This is why we carry out repeat readings in some investigations – to generate reliable data. Therefore, if you have large differences within sets of repeat readings, your data could be unreliable and you cannot place much trust in your conclusions.

You could also consider any patterns you spot – ask yourself 'are they likely to extend beyond the range of values you chose to investigate'?

If you do a 'pattern seeking' enquiry, especially those involving living things, you need to think about the size of the sample you choose. Is it large enough for you to be confident in your conclusions?

You want to gather trustworthy data that really helps you to answer your original question.

a How can you improve the reliability of your measurements in an investigation?

b i Work out the average (mean) result from this set of three repeat readings:
18 °C, 17 °C, 19 °C

ii What can you conclude about this set of data?

iii What measuring instrument was used to take these repeat readings?

c What is another word for 'reliable' in a scientific investigation?

d The passage above says to ask yourself if a pattern is likely to extend beyond the range of values you chose to investigate.
How could you check this out if you investigated the effect of hanging 10g, 20g, 30g and 40g on the end of a spring?

e A medical company was planning to test a new drug on volunteer patients. Which sample size would give the more reliable results – testing 20 patients or 2000 patients? Give a reason for your choice

4 A group was investigating cars rolling down a ramp.

They wanted to see how the angle of a slope affected the distance a car rolled.

The title of their investigation was phrased as a question.

a What is a possible title of the investigation?

b Using the list a–g in question 1, what type of enquiry would answer their question?

c What was the independent variable in their investigation.

d What was the dependent variable?

e Which variables did they have to control?

f What measuring instrument would they use to measure the dependent variable? Give the units of these measurements.

g How could they make their results more reliable?

2 Investigating matter

2.1 States of matter

Figure 2.1a Here we have a solid – the plastic of the bottle, a liquid – the fizzy drink, made up mainly of water, and a gas – the carbon dioxide gas trapped in the bubbles frothing out

What's the matter?

Practically everything around us is made of matter. **Anything that has mass and volume is made of matter.**

Classifying matter

In order to make sense of the natural world, scientists try to sort things out into groups. They classify matter as either:

● solid

● liquid, or

● gas.

These are known as the three states of matter.

Activity

Make a list

Look around you and make a list of the different materials (also called substances by scientists) you can see.

Do not write the name of the objects. For example, if you can see a chair, do not put 'chair', but the material from which it is made, such as 'wood' or 'plastic'.

Here is a summary of the properties of solids, liquids and gases:

	Does it have a fixed shape?	Is it easy to compress?	Does it spread out or flow easily?
Solid	yes	no	no
Liquid	no	no	yes
Gas	no	yes	yes

Particle theory

Scientists believe that all matter is made up of tiny, ball-shaped particles. These particles are too small to be seen.

We can explain the properties of solids, liquids and gases using the idea that matter is made of particles (called the particle theory).

Activity

Which state of matter?

Look at the list of materials (substances) you listed in the previous activity box.

Your task is to classify the materials in your list as solids, liquids or gases.

Create a poster or booklet to share your findings.

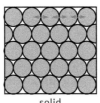 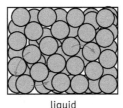 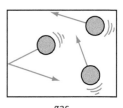

solid   liquid   gas

Figure 2.1b The arrangement of particles in a solid, liquid and gas

This table gives a summary of the arrangement and movement of the particles, as well as the forces between particles, in the three states of matter.

Properties	Solid	Liquid	Gas
Arrangement of particles	Particles packed closely together	Particles just slightly further apart than in a solid	Particles furthest apart on average – mainly empty space
Forces of attraction between particles	Strong	Weak	Very weak
Movement of particles	Very limited movement; they do vibrate	Random movement	Rapid, free movement

Key points

Matter is anything that has mass and volume.

Matter can exist in three different states – solids, liquids and gases.

The particle theory explains the behaviour of solids, liquids and gases.

Summary questions

1 Copy and complete:

Solids and liquids cannot be _____ easily, like a gas. A solid has a fixed _____ whereas liquids and gases take the _____ of their container. A gas will _____ out in all directions but solids _____ in one position.

2 Draw diagrams to show the different arrangement of particles in solids, liquids and gases.

3 Describe the different movement of the particles in a solid, liquid and gas.

4 Write a poem with the title 'Solids, liquids and gases'. Make sure you mention particles.

2.2 Diffusion

Figure 2.2a The sweet smell of perfume spreads through the air by diffusion

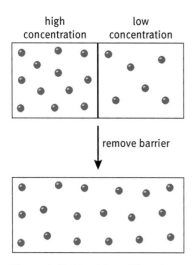

Figure 2.2b Particles diffuse from a high concentration to a low concentration

Do you like the smell of freshly baked bread? You can thank a process called diffusion for spreading the particles from the bread, through the air and into your nose.

Activity

Spreading out

Your teacher will pour some perfume or after-shave into a flat dish at the front of the room.

● Put your hand up when you can smell it.

● Discuss what happened, explaining your observations in terms of particles.

● Draw diagrams to show how the concentration of the particles changes.

Diffusion is the process whereby substances mingle and pass through each other, without us having to stir or mix the substances. It takes place because of the random motion of the particles in liquids and in gases.

As a result of diffusion, particles move from an area of high concentration to an area of low concentration.

Note that **a more concentrated solution has more particles in a given volume compared to a less concentrated solution.**

More evidence for diffusion

The following diffusion experiments provide evidence that the tiny particles the make up matter really do exist – even if we can't see them!

Diffusion through a gas

The experiment shown below shows how particles also diffuse through gases, as well as liquids. The liquids involved, concentrated ammonia solution and concentrated hydrochloric acid, are both corrosive. For this reason, this experiment should only be carried out as a teacher demonstration.

When the stoppers from both liquids are held near each other, white smoke is seen in the air. This happens because ammonia particles (evaporating from the ammonia solution) react with hydrogen chloride particles (from the hydrochloric acid). The reaction forms a fine white powder of a substance called ammonium chloride – which we see as the white smoke.

Activity

Diffusion through a liquid

Fill a beaker with water. Pick up a crystal of the dark purple substance, potassium manganate(VII) using a pair of tweezers.

Gently drop the crystal into the still water in the beaker.

Watch what happens for a few minutes, then leave it undisturbed to look at next lesson.

- Write down your observations.

- Explain your observations using the particle theory of matter.

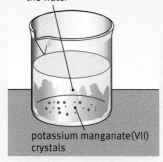

purple colour starts spreading through the water

potassium manganate(VII) crystals

Figure 2.2d Potassium manganate(VII) diffusing through water

The two liquids can be placed in a long tube as shown below:

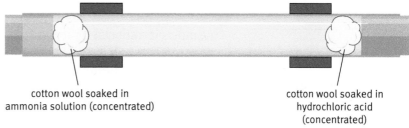

cotton wool soaked in ammonia solution (concentrated)

cotton wool soaked in hydrochloric acid (concentrated)

Figure 2.2c Diffusion through air

After leaving the tube a few minutes a ring of white smoke appears inside the long tube. This shows that particles of ammonia and hydrogen chloride must have travelled along the tube, even though we cannot see them – otherwise, how could the white smoke form inside the tube?

Key points

- Diffusion is the movement of particles from an area of high concentration to an area of low concentration.

- Diffusion takes place because of the random motion of the particles in liquids and gases.

Summary questions

1 Copy and complete using the words below:

low   stir   gases   high   move   diffusion

When substances mix automatically, without us having to _____ them, we call it _____. This happens because particles in liquids and _____ are able to _____ around in a random manner. The particles move from an area of _____ concentration to an area of _____ concentration.

2 Look at the experiment in the long tube shown in Figure 2.2c above

   a What is seen in the long tube where the acid and ammonia particles meet?

   b The reaction in the tube takes place nearer the end of the containing concentrated hydrochloric acid. So which particles diffuse faster, ammonia or hydrogen chloride particles from the acid?

2.3 Osmosis

Osmosis is a special type of diffusion. It involves the movement of water through a selectively or partially permeable membrane, such as cell membranes in your body. You can imagine a membrane as a very thin sheet with tiny holes in it. 'Selectively or partially permeable' means that only particles of certain substances can pass through the membrane.

Small particles, such as those of water, can pass through the membrane. However, large particles, such as those of sugar, cannot get through it. This is similar to what happens on a larger scale with a sieve or strainer – where only small pieces of material pass through the tiny holes.

The direction in which the water particles move depends on the concentration of water particles on either side of the membrane. We can think of a dilute solution as having a 'high concentration of water'. So water particles move from where their concentration is high, in a dilute solution, to where their concentration is low, in a more concentrated solution.

Note that the more water in a certain volume of solution, the more dilute the solution is.

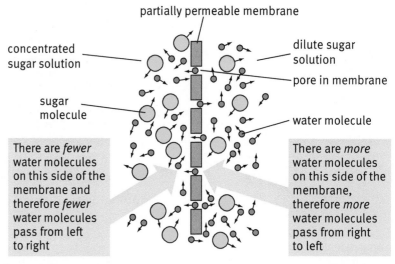

Figure 2.3a Osmosis is the movement of water across a partially permeable membrane

Osmosis in plants

We can study osmosis in experiments using pieces of fruit or vegetables because plant cells have partially permeable membranes. Now you can try the 'Looking at osmosis' experiment in the Activity box opposite.

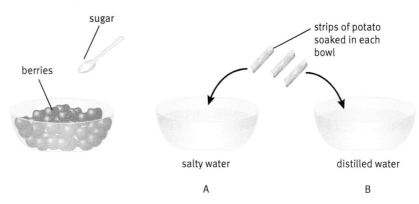

Figure 2.3b Osmosis experiments

Activity

Looking at osmosis

a Put berries into two bowls. Sprinkle sugar on one bowl of berries and leave both bowls overnight. Note your observations.

b Place identical strips of potato in a bowl of salty water (A) and in a bolw of distilled water (B). Leave overnight. Note your observations.

- Write up these experiments in the style shown in Module 1.

- Explain your observations using your ideas about osmosis.

The osmosis experiments can be explained by the movement of water into and out of the vacuole that occupies the centre of a plant cell (see page 73).

If the solution outside the plant cell is more concentrated than the solution in the plant's cells, then water will move out of the cells. This makes the cells shrink and shrivel up. They are then called flaccid cells. (It's a bit like a football that has gone soft as most of the air inside has escaped).When this happens the plants leaves start to curl up and wilt.

On the other hand, if the solution outside the plant cell is more dilute than the solution inside the cell, water moves into the cell. This has the effect of filling up the vacuole with solution. This makes the cells harder and more rigid. In this state they are described as being turgid. Turgid cells help to support the plant. (It's a bit like a football blown up with a pump, with extra air forced in).

Key points

- Osmosis is the movement of water particles across a selectively or partially permeable membrane.

- The water moves from a dilute solution, with a high concentration of water, to a concentrated solution, with a low concentration of water.

Summary questions

1 a What is a selectively/partially permeable membrane?

  b Where are selectively/partially permeable membranes found in the human body?

  c Which substance moves when osmosis occurs?

2 A bowl of red kidney beans that is left to soak overnight in distilled water will take a shorter time to soften during cooking than beans that were not soaked. Explain this using your ideas about osmosis.

2.4 Changes of state

Learning outcomes

At the end of this topic you should be able to:

▸ name and explain changes of state

▸ identify everyday changes of state.

Activity

The boiling point of water

Your task is to find the boiling point of water using common laboratory apparatus.

- Design an experiment and show it to your teacher before you start.

- Write up your experiment, including a diagram in your method. Use the headings shown in Module 1.

You are now aware that there are three states of matter – solid, liquid and gas. For a particular substance, whether it exists as a solid, liquid or gas depends on its temperature.

Water is a good example for us to examine.

- At temperatures of 0°C and below, it is usually a solid, that is called ice.

- At temperatures between 0°C and 100°C, it is mainly a liquid (water).

- At temperatures at and above 100°C, it is a gas that is called steam.

Heating up

- When ice turns to water, we say that it **melts**. Ice melts above 0°C.

- When liquid water turns to a gas, we say it **evaporates**. If the temperature is high enough, bubbles of steam will start forming in the water. They rise and burst through the surface of the water, allowing steam to escape. This is called **boiling**. Boiling is the change from a liquid to a gas which takes place at the boiling point of the liquid. The boiling point of water is 100°C

Some solids change directly into a gas, without passing through the liquid state. We say that the solid, such as iodine, **sublimes**. An everyday example is toilet bowl freshener, used in the home. The solid decreases in size as it changes to a gas which diffuses through the air to eliminate smells.

Cooling down

- When steam hits a cold surface, it turns from a gas back to liquid water. This happens on a mirror in a steamy bathroom when taking a hot water bath. We say that the steam **condenses** on the mirror. This also happens when the cover is removed from a saucepan in which food is being cooked in boiling water.

- When liquid water is cooled to 0°C it **freezes** to form solid ice.

We can summarise these changes of state as shown below:

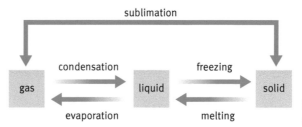

Figure 2.4a Changes of state

Why changes of state take place

Heating up

Temperature has an effect on the behaviour of particles in matter. How the particles behave brings about changes in the state of the substance.

- As we heat up a solid, its particles vibrate more and more quickly.
- Eventually, the particles shake about so much that they start to break free from each other.
- At this point the solid begins to melt and the shape of the solid breaks down.
- If we carry on heating, the particles in the liquid move around more quickly.
- Some particles at the surface have enough energy to escape the liquid as a gas.
- The liquid is evaporating. With more heating the liquid starts to boil.

Cooling down

- When the particles in a gas are cooled so that their temperature is decreased, their movement slows down.
- Eventually, the distance between the particles is small and the gas changes into a liquid.
- Further cooling of the liquid causes the particles to move around more slowly.
- They get closer together until they stay in fixed positions and form the regular shape of a solid.

Key points

- Melting describes the change of state from a solid to a liquid.
- A liquid changing to a gas is evaporation (or boiling if it happens at the boiling point).
- Condensation is the changing of a gas into a liquid.
- Freezing, sometimes called solidifying, is the change from a liquid to a solid.
- Sublimation is the change from a solid directly to a gas and the reverse of this change.

Summary questions

1 Draw a flow diagram to summarise all the changes of state.

2 Make a table showing which changes of state take place as their energy increases and which happen as their energy decreases.

Energy increases	Energy decreases

3 Make a table showing at least five examples of everyday changes of state. Next to each change, give the name of the change of state, for example melting.

Change of state	Example

2.5 Water

Learning outcomes

At the end of this topic you should be able to:

▸ explain why water is so important

▸ explain the water cycle.

Water is essential to life on Earth. In fact, more than 60% of your body is water. Water also provides the habitat (a place to live) for all aquatic animals, from whales to shrimps. These habitats can be seas, rivers, streams, lakes or ponds. Plants take in water through their roots and animals drink water.

Water is also an excellent solvent as it can dissolve many substances. This means that blood, which contains water, can carry dissolved substances around your body. It explains why we wash with water too, and use it to clean many other items in our lives.

Activity

Uses of water

Working in a group, carry out some research to find out about the uses of water.

Choose how to present your results to the rest of the class.

The water cycle

The water on Earth moves from place to place in a process called the water cycle. Energy from the Sun powers the water cycle, as shown in the diagram below:

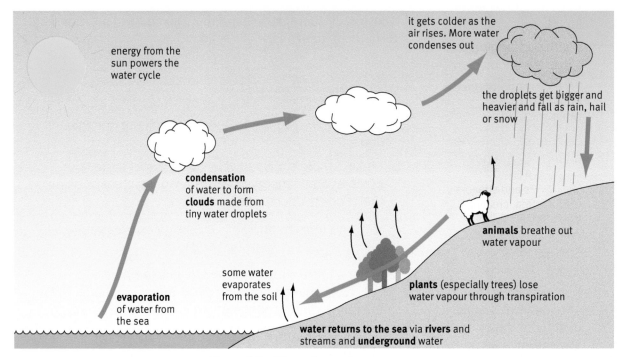

Figure 2.5a The water cycle

- Energy from the Sun helps water to evaporate from the sea.
- As it rises, the water vapour cools and condenses into tiny droplets of water which form clouds.

Figure 2.5b Clouds are made of condensed water

- When the clouds are forced to rise they get even colder and the droplets join together until they are too heavy to stay suspended in the air. The larger droplets fall as rain (or as hail or snow if the temperature is 0°C or below and the drops of water freeze). This is called precipitation.
- The water that falls on land can evaporate again directly from the ground and inland waterways or it is taken in by plants and animals.
- Alternatively, it returns to the sea in streams and rivers.
- Then the water cycle starts again.

Figure 2.5c Rivers and streams flow towards the sea, creating beautiful landscapes

Key points

- Water is important for drinking, dissolving substances, cooling (in industry and in animals) and as the major compound in the human body.
- The main changes of state in the water cycle are evaporation and condensation. Freezing and melting are also involved.

Summary questions

1 Make a list of ten uses of water.

2 Draw a flow diagram to explain the water cycle.

3 In which parts of the water cycle are the following changes of state found:

  a condensation   c freezing

  b evaporation   d melting.

2.6 Investigating water

Learning outcome

At the end of this topic you should be able to:

▸ carry out investigations to show the physical properties of water.

The physical properties of water

Activity

Observing a sample of pure water

Place a little distilled water on a watch glass.

- How would you describe the colour of water?
- What about its smell?

Use a dropping pipette to carefully place a single drop of water on a sheet of plastic.

- Does the water spread out? Describe what you see.

We are all familiar with water as we use it every day, so we are aware of some of its properties although we might take them for granted. We can start by listing its more obvious properties.

Scientists describe the colour of water as 'colourless' (being without colour).

Water is a clear liquid, which means light can pass through it. However, we do not use 'clear' to describe its colour. There are many liquids that are clear, but are also coloured – just think of some drinks you can buy. So water can be described as a colourless liquid. Water also has no smell. Scientists describe it as 'odourless'.

The fact that water forms drops is interesting. We say that water has a high surface tension. We explain surface tension by thinking about the forces between neighbouring particles at the surface of water. In water these forces are quite strong. This attraction results in a type of invisible skin across the surface of water.

Look at Figure 2.6a:

Did you know?

A droplet of water can hang from the underside of a roof for a long time due to surface tension and forces of attraction between the water particles.

Figure 2.6a Water has a high surface tension

The next activity is one way to show the high surface tension of water.

Figure 2.6b This insect uses the high surface tension of water to move across the pond

Activity

The surface tension of water

Your task is to float a needle on the surface of a bowl of water.

Gently place a needle lying on a piece of filter paper (or tissue paper) on the surface of the water.

As the paper gets wet it will sink and the needle should be left floating on top of the water.

The high surface tension of water keeps the needle afloat – even though the density of the metal should cause the needle to sink.

On page 32 you carried out an experiment to find the boiling point of distilled water. Now you can carry out another experiment to find its freezing and melting point.

Activity

Melting/freezing point of water

Fill a test tube to one third with distilled water. Use a thermometer to take its temperature.

Place the test tube and thermometer in a beaker containing a mixture of ice and salt. The ice/salt mixture will cool the water in the test tube down.

Record the temperature at regular intervals as it cools down and forms ice.

- Write up your experiment, including a diagram in your method, as well as a table and graph in your results.
- What is the freezing point and melting point of water?

Did you know?

Figure 2.6c You can get temperatures below 0 °C by mixing salt with ice – useful for keeping your ice cream cool

Hand crank ice cream coolers (like the one in the Figure 2.6c) are still common in some Caribbean islands. Ice and salt are packed around the inner ice cream container because salt lowers the freezing point of water. The result is that the ice cream is cooled faster and has a smoother and more creamy texture.

Continued

Figure 2.6d Dissolving sugar is an important part of the refining of the sugar from sugar cane.

Water as a solvent

A solvent is a liquid that dissolves other substances. Carry out the investigation below to find out more about water acting as a solvent.

Carry out the investigation below to find out more about water acting as a solvent for sugar.

Activity

Investigating sugar dissolving in water

In this investigation you will be guided through the process needed to plan your investigation, collect the data, and analyse it.

a List all the factors that you think might affect how quickly sugar dissolves.

b Decide which one of these factors you will investigate, then copy and complete the sentence below:

In our fair test we plan to see how .... affects how quickly sugar dissolves.

c Now start thinking about how to carry out your investigation.

Copy and complete:

We will change (our independent variable): ....

We will measure (our dependent variable): The time it takes the sugar to dissolve in water

We will keep these things the same (the control variables): ....

d You will have to record your times for sugar to dissolve in a table.

Draw a table like the one below, filling in the variable you are investigating at the top of the 1st column. The number of rows depends on how many tests you plan to carry out.

	Time to dissolve (s)

If you intend to repeat each test to check your results, then you can divide up the 2nd column into the number of repeats and add an extra column for the average (mean) value calculated for each test.

Temperature of water (°C)	Time for sugar to dissolve (s)			
	1st test	2nd test	3rd test	Mean

e Think about how you will show your results from your table on a graph.

The independent variable you chose to investigate will go along the bottom axis of the graph.

The time it takes the sugar to dissolve (in seconds) will go up the side of your graph.

The graph will be a bar chart if your independent variable is described in words, for example, the type of sugar ('brown', 'white', 'sugar cubes', castor sugar'). In this case there would be four bars on your bar chart.

On the other hand, the graph will be a line graph if your independent variable is measured. For example, if you change the temperature of the water in each test.

f After collecting your data and drawing your graph. Describe any pattern in your results.

For example – 'As we increased the ……, the time it took the sugar to dissolve increased/decreased.

Then try to explain why, using your ideas about particles.

g At this stage write an evaluation of your investigation, suggesting and explaining any ways in which you could have improved your investigation.

When you have carried out the sugar dissolving investigation you can try the investigation below, making more of the decisions yourself.

Activity

What affects how quickly salt dissolves in water?

Think of as many variables as you can that might affect how quickly salt dissolves in water.

Choose one of these variables to investigate. Make a prediction and plan your investigation.

Allow your teacher to check your plan before you start the practical work.

Write up the completed investigation.

Key point

- Water is an odourless, colourless liquid, with a high surface tension.
- The melting point of water is 0 °C and its boiling point is 100 °C.
- Water is an excellent solvent for many substances.

Summary questions

1 Make a list of the physical properties of pure water.

2 Explain the following observations:

a A thin film of water appears on the OUTSIDE of a glass filled with ice and water.

b Rain forms droplets on a pane of glass.

2.7 Water and pollution

Many uses of water rely on its ability to dissolve other substances. This useful property becomes a disadvantage when harmful waste products from homes and industry enter waterways, dissolve and cause pollution of water. Harmful substances in our environment are called **pollutants**. We can find pollutants in oceans, seas, rivers, creeks and lakes.

Figure 2.7a These brown lagoons in Jamaica are caused by waste iron oxide from bauxite mined for the extraction of aluminium metal

Pollutants dissolved in water

Examples of pollutants in our waterways include raw sewage from farms and from accidents at sewage works. Fertilisers also cause pollution when they are washed from the soil by rainwater and flow into waterways. These pollutants can kill the animals that live in the water and rely on water for the dissolved oxygen gas it contains.

The fertilisers and sewage, as well as waste detergents, encourage plant growth in the water. A covering of algae forms on the surface. The oxygen gets used up by microorganisms who feed on the algae when they die. This results in very little oxygen dissolving in the water for the animals and plants which live below the surface

Figure 2.7b You can see the algae covering the surface of this waterway affected by excess fertiliser being washed out of the soil on farmland

Activity

How clean is your water?

Look at a sample of water from a local waterway.

Comment on the colour, smell and cloudiness (also known as turbidity) of the water sample.

Key points

- Water can be polluted by sewage, fertilisers or detergents, which promote the growth of algae and eventually results in the death of aquatic animals.

- Water taken from a river to cool down machines in a factory and returned to the river at a higher temperature affects the balance of aquatic life.

- Soil washed off hills by heavy rains in deforested areas can cause silting up in rivers and cloudiness in seawater which adversely affects coral reefs.

Farming can also result in pesticides entering our waterways. These toxic chemicals can build up (accumulate) in the bodies of living things in a food chain. The larger aquatic animals, at the top of the food chain, suffer as they eat many water plants and smaller animals to survive, resulting in large amounts of toxic chemicals entering, and staying in, their bodies.

Thermal pollution

As well as being used as a solvent, water is also used as a coolant in industry. For example, in power stations cold water in pipes is used to cool down steam to cause it to change into water. The warm water is then released into a nearby river. This can cause the temperature of the river to rise, disrupting the delicate balance of life. This is called thermal pollution.

Soil erosion by rainwater

In some places, land is cleared of natural forests to provide more land for farming. On sloping land, the trees roots help to keep the soil in place. Once the trees are removed (called deforestation) heavy rain can wash the topsoil away. When this land becomes unable to produce crops, often more land is then cleared of forest. This destroys the habitat of yet more wildlife.

The fine particles of soil, called silt, get washed down to rivers and creeks. The waters turn cloudy, affecting the hatching of fish eggs. Deposited silt also raises river beds, increasing the risk of flooding. If the silt is carried by the river out to sea, the cloudy water has a harmful effect on coral reefs. These precious ecosystems are easily destroyed and take long periods of time to be replaced.

Summary questions

1 Make a list of pollutants that can find their way into water.

2 How can rainwater indirectly cause harm to a coral reef many miles away from the place it falls?

3 Carry out research to find out how the following affects our environment:

   a Oil spills

   b Waste from cruise ships.

Use the information collected to create a poster, booklet, poem or other method to share with others in your class.

2.8 Atoms

Did you know?

There are only 92 different types of atom found naturally on Earth. Your body is made up from just 26 types of different atom.

Activity

Research objects in which the elements listed in the table opposite are important. The results of your research may be brief statements, such as: aluminum is used to make pots and pans; tungsten is used in the filaments of light bulbs; copper is used to make electric wires.

Scientists believe that everything is made up from tiny particles. These particles are too small to see directly. So scientists have had to think up ideas which explain the things they can see.

Over 200 years ago a scientist called John Dalton put forward his ideas. He thought that the particles were like tiny versions of the hard balls used to play pool. They could not be split. He called them **atoms**. So atoms are the *smallest units or pieces of matter*.

Dalton suggested that there were just a few dozen different types of atom. The atoms could join together in different combinations to make new substances (just like you can combine letters in the alphabet to form different words). Many of Dalton's ideas are still useful today.

Chemical symbols

Each atom has its own name and chemical symbol. Most symbols are taken from the English names, but others are based on their Latin names.

Look at the table below. Notice that you always use a capital letter for the first letter of a symbol. If the symbol has a second letter, it is always a small letter. Examples include Cu, Fe and Ne.

Atom	Symbol	Atom	Symbol
aluminium	Al	mercury	Hg
calcium	Ca	neon	Ne
carbon	C	nitrogen	N
chlorine	Cl	oxygen	O
copper	Cu	platinum	Pt
fluorine	F	potassium	K
gold	Au	silicon	Si
helium	He	silver	Ag
hydrogen	H	sodium	Na
iodine	I	sulphur	S
Iron	Fe	titanium	Ti
Lead	Pb	tungsten	W
magnesium	Mg	zinc	Zn

Inside the atom

About 100 years ago scientists found that each individual particle could be made up of three types of smaller 'sub-atomic' particles.

These are:

● protons

● neutrons

● electrons.

The protons and neutrons are found squashed up together in the centre of the atom. The centre is called the nucleus, It is incredibly small and dense.

The tiny electrons whizz around the nucleus.

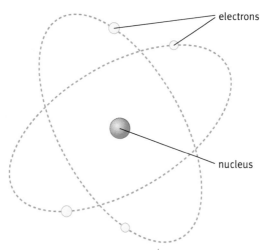

electrons

nucleus

Figure 2.8a This model of the atom was suggested by scientists about a century ago but is still useful today

Summary questions

1 Define an atom.

2 Using the table of chemical symbols on the previous page, answer the following questions:

   a Name and give the symbols of the atoms whose symbol is the same as the first letter of their name in English.

   b Name and give the symbols of the atoms that have symbols based on their Latin names.

   c Why is helium's symbol He, and not H?

   d Cobalt has the symbol Co. Why would scientists fail to recognise it if someone made a mistake and wrote it as CO?

3 Draw a labelled diagram to show the structure of the atom.

2.9 Developing ideas about atoms

In science, ideas used to explain why things happen change as time passes and new observations are made. If the new ideas are better at explaining things than the existing idea, scientists will eventually change their old ideas and accept the new ones. This is how our ideas about atoms developed over time.

Democritus

The ancient Greeks were the first people to suggest that everything is made of tiny particles. The Greeks were great thinkers about the world they lived in, although they didn't bother much with experiments. A Greek philosopher called Democritus put forward his model to explain the way materials behave.

He believed that everything was made of particles. The particles he talked about were so small that you couldn't see them.

Democritus could explain the different properties of substances by relating them to the size and shape of their particles. For example, he imagined that particles in a hard, strong metal, such as iron, must be jagged at the edges so that they could be jammed into position next to each other. On the other hand particles in water were probably smooth and round in shape so they could flow over each other.

But by the start of the 1800s, science was more firmly based on observation and experiments. A scientist called John Dalton, who taught in Manchester (United Kingdom), loved experimenting. His careful experiments suggested to him that all matter is made up of tiny particles that could not be broken down into anything smaller. He called the particles 'atoms', as used by the ancient Greeks.

He drew up a list of elements – substances that were made of only one type of atom and couldn't be broken down into simpler substances. He visualised atoms as hard, indestructible spheres. He suggested that each element has atoms of a different mass.

A list of Dalton's elements is shown in Figure 2.9b.

In the 1890s an English scientist called J.J. Thomson was experimenting with gases at low pressure inside electric discharge tubes. He discovered a new type of particle that appeared to have a very small mass. In fact there must be thousands of them inside each atom, thought Thomson, to explain the mass of an atom. The negatively charged particles he discovered are called **electrons**. Look at his model of the atom shown in Figure 2.9c on the next page, devised to explain his observations.

Then in 1910 two young researchers, Geiger and Marsden were making use of recently discovered radioactive particles to investigate atoms. They fired alpha particles (relatively heavy, positively charged particles) at a thin piece of gold foil.

Figure 2.9a Democritus was a wealthy Greek philosopher, born in 460 BC. He has been commemorated on Greek stamps and has a large research institute near Athens named after him.

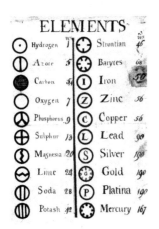

Figure 2.9b John Dalton's list of elements and the symbols he gave them.

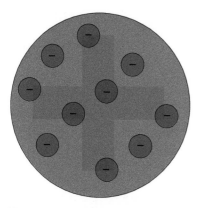

Figure 2.9c This is what Thomson thought an atom must be like.

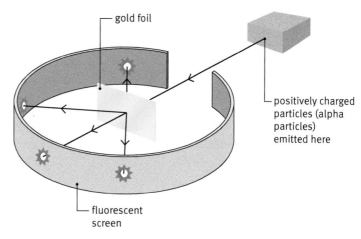

Figure 2.9d This was the experiment that led to the idea that atoms have a nucleus.

Assuming Thomson's model of the atom, they had expected most of the heavy, positively charged alpha particles to barge straight through the atoms of gold. After all, the positive charge was spread out over the whole atom in a 'cloud'. However, few of the alpha particles actually bounced back.

To explain these results, Rutherford suggested that the positive charge and mass of an atom was concentrated into a very small area at the centre of an atom. We call this the **nucleus** of the atom. He imagined that the electrons were orbiting the nucleus, a bit like the planets around the Sun. Look back at Figure 2.8a to see Rutherfords nuclear model of the atom.

Since then there have been many new things discovered about atoms but you can learn more about those if you go on to study science at a higher level.

Key points

- Our understanding about atoms has developed over time.

- Observations from experiments led scientsists to accept that atoms have a positively charged nucleus, with negatively charge electrons orbiting around it.

Summary questions

1 a Name the ancient Greek who put forward the idea about matter being made up of particles.

   b Describe how he explained that water can flow from one place to another.

2 What did J.J. Thomson discover?

3 Describe Rutherford's nuclear model of the atom and include a diagram in your answer.

2.10 Elements, compounds and mixtures

Elements

Elements are substances that contain only *one type of atom*.

There are only 92 elements on Earth that occur naturally. They are listed by chemists in the Periodic Table.

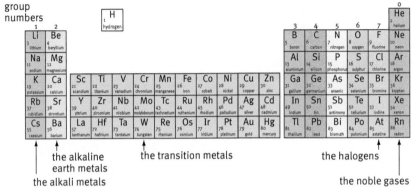

Figure 2.10a The Periodic Table of chemical elements

Compounds

Compounds are substances made up of two or more different types of atom that are chemically combined together.

The atoms in compounds are chemically bonded to each other and are difficult to separate again.

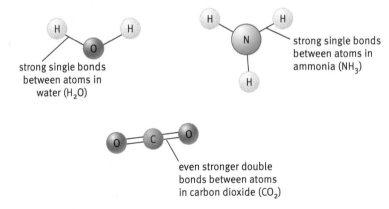

strong single bonds between atoms in water (H_2O)

strong single bonds between atoms in ammonia (NH_3)

even stronger double bonds between atoms in carbon dioxide (CO_2)

Figure 2.10b Examples of three common compounds

The properties of a compound are totally different from those of the elements it contains. For example, sodium is a very reactive metal; chlorine is a toxic gas; these two elements combine chemically to form sodium chloride – which is table salt. Fortunately, table salt is nothing like its elements, sodium or chlorine!

Figure 2.10c Compounds have different properties from the elements they contain

Mixtures

Mixtures contain two or more elements (and/or compounds) that have been physically combined together. There are no chemical bonds between the different substances in the mixture so they can be separated again quite easily.

Many of the substances we use in everyday life are mixtures rather than pure substances. Examples include cosmetics, paints, aerosols, alloys (mixtures of metals) and cleaning products. Most drinks are mixtures, such as milk, lime juice or coconut water.

The example below shows the difference between elements, mixtures and compounds.

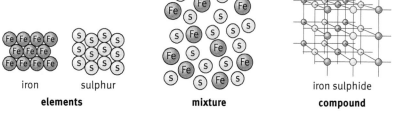

iron   sulphur

elements   **mixture**   iron sulphide

compound

Figure 2.10d Distinguishing between an element, a mixture and a compound

Key points

- Elements contain only one type of atom.

- Compounds contain two or more different types of atom. These are difficult to separate into elements.

- Mixtures contain two or more different substances physically combined, with no chemical bonds between the different substances. These are quite easy to separate.

Summary questions

1 Define the following:

a an element   b a compound   c a mixture.

2 Sort the following substances out into elements, mixtures and compounds and show your results in a table:

salt   hydrogen   water   milk   copper sulphate   mercury   ammonia   seawater carbon dioxide   paint   brass

3 Why should advertisers NOT describe mineral water as 'pure water'?

4 Describe an experiment that could show that salty water is a mixture.

2.11 Solutions and suspensions

At the end of this topic you should be able to:

▸ to classify some mixtures as solutions and some as suspensions

▸ to use evaporation to separate a mixture.

Activity

Distinguishing between a solution and a suspension

Stir a little chalk dust into half a beaker of water.

Do the same thing with table salt and water.

Place the mixtures next to each other in front of a light source.

Now try looking through each mixture at the light.

What do you notice?

Solutions

Sugar is a **soluble** solid. This means that when you add sugar to water and stir the mixture, it dissolves and you can no longer see the solid bits of sugar. You have made a mixture that is a **solution** of sugar in water. The solid that dissolves in a solution is called the **solute** and the liquid it dissolves in is the **solvent**.

The crystals of sugar dissolve when the individual particles have separated because they are attracted by water particles. The individual particles of sugar and other compounds are called **molecules**. A molecule is a group of two or more atoms chemically bonded together.

The sugar molecules are spread throughout the molecules of water. This explains why the water has a sweet taste or changes colour (with brown sugar). Even when we stop stirring they remain mixed up together because of the random motion of the molecules in the liquid mixture (solution).

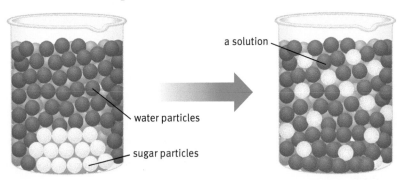

Figure 2.11a The sugar molecules get spread throughout the water to make a sugar solution

In a solution the particles (or molecules) are so small that they cannot be filtered out of the solution even using the finest filter paper.

Suspensions

Some solids are **insoluble**. This means that they do not dissolve in water. The mixture formed is called a suspension. A **suspension** is a mixture of small bits of an insoluble solid spread throughout water, or any other liquid. Stirring up mud in water makes a suspension.

Solutions are described as 'clear' liquids. Light can pass straight through a solution.

However, suspensions appear cloudy. Light is scattered in all directions off the tiny pieces of solid in the mixture.

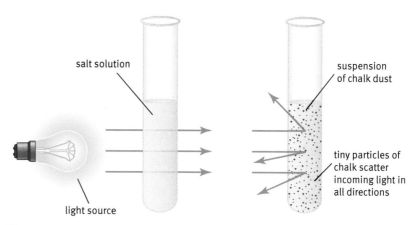

Figure 2.11b Solutions allow light to pass through them and appear clear, unlike suspensions

Separating a solid from a solution

We can separate a dissolved solid from its solution by **evaporation**. If the solution is heated, water evaporates off and the dissolved solid is left behind.

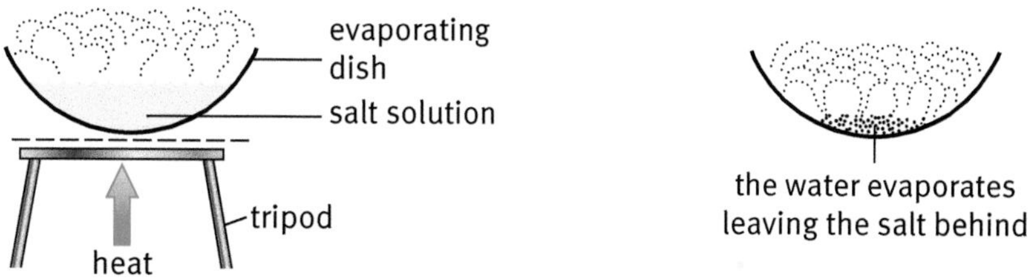

Figure 2.11c Separating solids from seawater

Seawater is a mixture of water and different dissolved salts. These salts are collected in salt-pans. The seawater is run into shallow pools and energy from the Sun evaporates off the water. The salts are then collected to sell.

Activity

Heating seawater

Watch your teacher heat some seawater.

Describe what happens in the experiment.

Key points

- A solution is a mixture of a dissolved substance (or substances) in a solvent (liquid).
- A suspension is a mixture of fine particles of insoluble solid spread throughout a liquid.
- We can separate a dissolved solid from a solution by evaporating off the water.

Summary questions

1. What is a solution? Draw a diagram to help your explanation.
2. What is a suspension?
3. Make a table showing which of the following mixtures are solutions and which are suspensions:

   seawater **muddy water** **chalky water** **sugary drink**
4. How can you distinguish between a solution and a suspension?

The ways in which we separate mixtures depends on differences between the properties of its components (individual substances).

Filtration

To separate an insoluble solid from a liquid we use **filtration**:

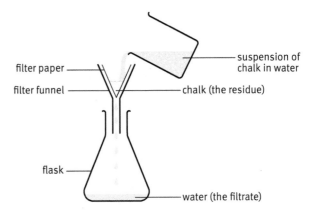

filter paper

filter funnel

suspension of chalk in water

chalk (the residue)

flask

water (the filtrate)

Figure 2.12a Filtration

This technique is used to filter fresh coffee.

Decanting

Some liquids, like oil and water, do not mix. They form two separate layers. The liquids are said to be immiscible. To separate one liquid from a mixture of two immiscible liquids, decanting is used. We use a separating funnel to decant the liquid.

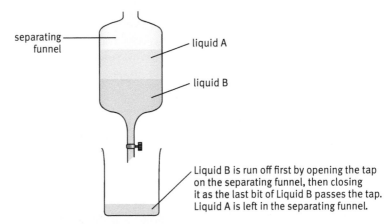

separating funnel

liquid A

liquid B

Liquid B is run off first by opening the tap on the separating funnel, then closing it as the last bit of Liquid B passes the tap. Liquid A is left in the separating funnel.

Figure 2.12b Decanting using a separating funnel

We can also decant a liquid from above a sediment of insoluble solids settled on the bottom of a container. This technique is used to separate vintage wines from any sediment in their bottles.

If the insoluble solid and liquid form a suspension, we can centrifuge the mixture first. In a centrifuge machine, the suspension is spun around at high speed. The insoluble solid particles are forced to the bottom of the test tube. Then the liquid above can be poured off. This is done to separate the cells from the liquid in a sample of blood.

Simple distillation

We have seen how a solid can be separated from a solution by evaporation on page 49. But say we want to collect the liquid from the solution and not just let it evaporate away into the air. We can do this using simple distillation, which requires a piece of apparatus called a condenser:

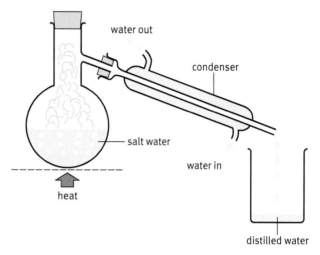

Figure 2.12c Simple distillation

The vapour from the solution is cooled down in the condenser. The gas condenses and turns back to liquid so that the solvent can be collected. This technique is used in desalination where seawater is converted to water that we can drink and use in the home or industry. In desalination plants the seawater is boiled under reduced pressure. This lowers the boiling point and uses less energy.

Key points

- Filtering can separate an insoluble solid from a liquid.

- Decanting can separate a liquid from a mixture of a liquid and an insoluble solid. It is also used to separate immiscible liquids.

- Simple distillation can separate and collect a liquid from a solution.

Summary questions

1 How would you separate the substance in bold from the mixture?

   a **Copper sulphate crystals** from copper sulphate solution.

   b **Petrol** from water and petrol.

   c **Soil** from muddy water.

   d **Water** from ink.

2 a What does 'desalination' mean?

   b Explain how the process of distillation works.

2.13 More methods of separation

Chromatography

We can separate the components in a mixture of dissolved substances using chromatography. In this method a drop of the mixture is placed onto a piece of filter paper or special chromatography paper. The paper is placed into a solvent, such as water or alcohol, which separates the different components in the mixture.

This separation technique depends on the different solubility of each of the dissolved component of the mixture. The more soluble the substance is in the solvent, the further up the paper it is carried by the solvent.

Activity

Detecting dyes in food colourings

In this experiment you can make a chromatogram to analyse various food colourings.

Use a thin capillary tube to dab spots of each food colouring on a pencil line, drawn near the bottom of a sheet of absorbent chromatography paper.

Then place the paper in a layer of water (the solvent) at the bottom of a beaker or tank.. Make sure that the level of the water is below the pencil line to start with.

Allow the water to soak up the paper, running past the spots of mixture.

Leave your paper (called a chromatogram) to dry in a warm place.

What can you deduce from your chromatography experiment?

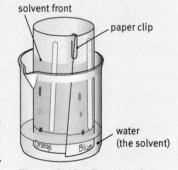

Figure 2.13a Running the chromatogram

Applications of chromatography

We can use chromatography to identify unknown substances by comparing the spots on a chromatogram with the spots from known substances. It is used by medical scientists in hospitals and in forensic scientists in police work.

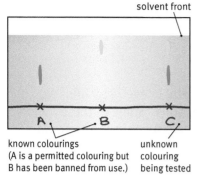

solvent front

known colourings
(A is a permitted colouring but
B has been banned from use.)

unknown
colouring
being tested

Figure 2.13b This is a chromatogram of an unknown colouring C and two known colourings A and B.

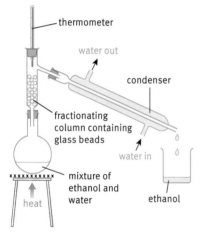

thermometer

water out

condenser

fractionating
column containing
glass beads

water in

mixture of
ethanol and
water

heat

ethanol

Figure 2.13c Fractional distillation is used to separate liquids with similar boiling points

Look at the chromatogram in Figure 2.13b.

The chromagram in Figure 2.13b shows that colouring C should be banned from use as it contains the safe colouring A but also the banned colouring B.

Sometimes the spots on the chromatogram are colourless so can't be seen directly. In these cases, scientists can use locating agents. These are sprayed on to the chromatogram and are designed to react with the substances in the spots to make coloured substances that can be seen.

Fractional distillation

We have already seen how we can use simple distillation to separate and collect a liquid from a solution (see Topic 2.12). However, if we have two liquids that have similar temperatures simple distillation does not give a good result. The distillate collected will still have a mixture of both liquids in it.

However, by adding a fractionating column above the flask being heated we can improve the separation of the two liquids. Look at Figure 2.13c.

The mixture of liquids is heated up to the boiling point of the liquid that boils first. At this temperature, vapour from both liquids will be rising up the fractionating column. However, the liquid with the higher boiling point will condense on the glass beads and fall back down into the flask below.

Key points

- Chromatography can separate dissolved solids from a solution, such as inks or dyes.

- Fractional distillation is used to separate liquids with similar boiling points.

Summary questions

1 Substance X is carried further up a chromatogram than substance Y. What does this tell us about the solubility of substances X and Y in the solvent used?

2 A food colouring is made up using a mixture of three natural dyes – red, yellow and blue. A food scientist ran a chromatogram of the food colouring using alcohol as a solvent. The blue dye was most soluble in alcohol and the red dye was least soluble. Draw the chromatogram you would expect the food scientist to develop.

3 Ethanol and water are two liquids that mix very well together. They do not form two separate layers. Ethanol's boiling point is 78 °C and water's is 100 °C. What would be the best method to separate a mixture of ethanol and water?

2.14 Metals and non-metals

Learning outcomes

At the end of this topic you should be able to:

▶ name some common metals and non-metals

▶ list the properties of metals and of non-metals

▶ classify substances as metals or non-metals.

Properties of metals

Many properties of metals are very useful in everyday life. We make a great variety of objects from metals. Some of these metals are elements, such as iron and zinc, and appear in the periodic table (see page 46). Others are mixtures of metals, called alloys, such as steel and brass.

Figure 2.14a shows the general properties of metals:

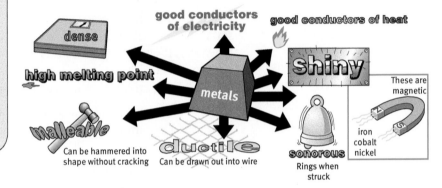

dense

good conductors of electricity

good conductors of heat

high melting point

shiny

metals

These are magnetic

iron cobalt nickel

malleable Can be hammered into shape without cracking

ductile Can be drawn out into wire

sonorous Rings when struck

Figure 2.14a The general properties of metals

Figure 2.14b The steel drums can be hammered into different shapes (as metals are **malleable**) to produce their different sounds (as metals are **sonorous**). Steel is an alloy of iron and carbon.

The element copper is a metal. It is a very good conductor of electricity and it is can be drawn out into wires (it is ductile). Therefore we use copper for electrical wiring in houses.

Properties of non-metals

There are many non-metallic substances that we use in our everyday lives. A few of these are elements, such as carbon in the form of diamond or graphite, but most are compounds or mixtures of compounds, such as plastics or wood.

Their properties are very varied. Although metals are all good conductors of electricity, most non-metallic materials are not. So we use non-metallic materials as electrical insulators. Electrical insulators do not allow electricity to pass through. We also use them as thermal insulators, especially if gas is trapped inside a foam. Figure 2.14b shows some general properties of non-metallic elements:

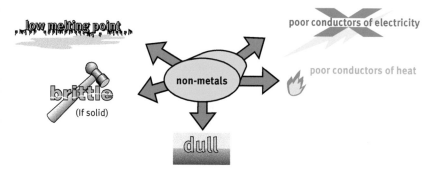

Figure 2.14c The general properties of non-metals

Wood

Wood is a useful naturally occurring material. There are many different types of wood. They vary from soft, low density balsa wood to hard, dense mahogany. Wood can be split along its grain, as when chopping firewood. However, it is much tougher to cut across its grain.

The fact that wood can be cut with metal saws, but is still a tough material makes it very useful. It is used to make homes and furniture, as well as fencing.

Plastics

Many plastics are synthetic (man-made) materials. There are lots of different types of plastics that can be manufactured. Their properties will depend on the starting materials used, the conditions used in the reaction to make them, how the plastic is processed.

Some plastics are flexible and melt or soften at low temperatures. These are used to make bags for carrying groceries. They can be recycled and remoulded to make new objects.

Other plastics are hard, rigid and heat resistant. These are used to make electrical plugs and sockets, as well as garbage cans and storage containers.

Activity

Classifying materials

Classify the following materials into metals and non-metals. Include pictures to demonstrate their uses:

- Lead
- Tin
- Pine
- Polythene
- Ceramic
- Fibre-glass
- Brass
- Nylon

Put your results in a table.

Key points

- In general, metals are good conductors of electricity and heat. They have high melting points, and are hard, dense, malleable, ductile, sonorous and shiny (**lustrous**).

- In general, non-metallic materials have relatively low densities, are soft, poor conductors of electricity and heat, dull and brittle.

Summary questions

1 Draw a table to show the general properties of metallic and non-metallic materials.

2 Which property would you choose to distinguish between a metal and a non-metal? Explain your answer.

3 Using the periodic table on page 46, make a table showing five elements which are metals and five elements which are non-metals. Give reasons for your answers.

2.15 Uses of metals and non-metals

Uses of metals

Can you imagine life without metals? Just think of all the things we rely on that are made from metals. Think of some of the things around your home that are made of metal. Did you include all the wiring, your water tank, or your cutlery and pans? Do you know which metals these things are made from?

Look at some of the metals found in homes shown below:

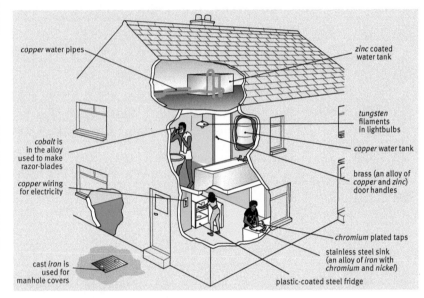

Figure 2.15a Metals are used in many ways in the home

Iron is the most commonly used metal, mostly as steels. Steels are alloys of iron with carbon. By varying the small amount of carbon mixed with iron in steel, we can change its properties. For instance, low-carbon steel can be pressed into different shapes so is used to make car bodies. On the other hand, high-carbon steel is much harder and is used to make drills and hammers.

Uses of non-metallic materials

The non-metallic materials can have a wide variety of properties so we have found many different uses for them. In the construction industry we have:

● bricks made from clay
● concrete made from small stones, cement sand and water
● glass made from sand limestone and soda lime
● PVC – a type of plastic
● wood of all types.

Concrete is the main material used in building in the world. It sets like a rock and is very strong, especially if reinforced with iron rods.

Exceptional properties

Most metals have high melting and boiling points. However, there is one particular exception – mercury. Mercury is a metal that is a liquid at room temperature (it has a low melting point). It is used inside thermometers.

An exceptional non-metals is carbon. Carbon exists as:

- graphite, which is a form of carbon that conducts electricity
- diamond, which is another form of carbon that is the hardest substance found on Earth.

Silicon is another strange non-metal as it is shiny and is a semi-conductor. It conducts electricity, but not as well as a metal or graphite.

Activity

The best material

Imagine you work for an advertising agency. You have been assigned to promote a certain material to the public. You will need to create a single-sided flyer that will be sent to households across the Caribbean.

Select any product you like and use the flyer to persuade the public of its benefits compared with a product made of an alternative, traditional type of material.

Key points

- Metals and non-metals have particular properties that we make use of in everyday life.
- There are some elements that do not share the general properties of metals or non-metals, such as the strange metal mercury.

Summary questions

1 Name the most useful property of a metal chosen for the following uses:

  a wires inside a set of head-phones

  b cooking pans

  c steel drums used in a band

  d wire fencing

  e jewellery.

2 Why do many people use plastic drainpipes rather than iron ones?

3 Give an advantage and a disadvantage of using polythene to make food bags rather than paper bags.

2.16 Acids and bases

Acids all around us

Many people think of acids as fuming, corrosive liquids which are very dangerous. But not all acids behave like this. We all use, and even eat, acids every day. For example, vinegar (which we use to make pepper sauce or to marinate meat) has the sharp, sour taste of acids. It contains ethanoic acid.

Citric acid gives oranges and lemons their sharp taste. These fruits also contain ascorbic acid. We know it better as vitamin C.

Figure 2.16a The sting of this ant contains formic acid. This is why ant stings hurt and itch. The acid irritates the skin.

Even the purest rainwater is slightly acidic. Carbon dioxide gas dissolves in the rain as it falls, making it acidic. This is also the gas in fizzy drinks, such as cola, beer and sparkling mineral water. These are all examples of weak acids that we meet every day.

Acids in school

You will have used acids in your science lessons. The 3 common acids found in schools are:

● hydrochloric acid, HCl

● sulphuric acid, H_2SO_4

● nitric acid, HNO_3

Note that chemical formula tells us the number of each type of atom in a molecule. So a molecule of HCl has one atom of hydrogen and one chlorine. No number following a symbol means '1'. An H_2SO_4 molecule contains 2 atoms of hydrogen, 1 atom of sulphur and 4 atoms of oxygen.

These are all strong acids. They can damage your skin so handle them with care.

Common bases

Bases react with acids to form compounds called salts, and also produce water in the reaction.

Metal oxides and hydroxides tend to be bases. Examples are magnesium oxide and sodium hydroxide. Many bases are insoluble in water.

However, if a base does dissolve in water, we call it an alkali. Examples of soluble bases are sodium oxide and potassium oxide. When these dissolve they make solutions of hydroxides (sodium hydroxide solution and potassium hydroxide solution). These alkaline solutions feel soapy to the touch, but can also be corrosive.

Examples of bases, and their chemical formulae, include:

- Sodium hydroxide, NaOH
- Potassium hydroxide, KOH
- Ammonia solution (sometimes referred to as ammonium hydroxide), NH_4OH
- Magnesium hydroxide, $Mg(OH)_2$
- Calcium hydroxide, $Ca(OH)_2$

Key points

- Acids form sour tasting solutions.
- Bases react with acids to form a salt and water.
- Bases that dissolve in water are called alkalis. They form alkaline solutions.

Summary questions

1 How would you describe the taste of an acid?
2 What would an alkaline solution feel like if rubbed between a person's thumb and fingers?
3 What is the difference between a base and an alkali?
4 Draw a table showing three acids and three alkalis, together with their chemical formulae.

2.17 Measuring pH

Learning outcomes

At the end of this topic you should be able to:

▸ distinguish acidic and alkaline solutions

▸ use the pH scale to classify some common household products

▸ draw the pH scale from 0 to 14.

Did you know?

The petals of some flowers such as Hibiscus, Rose and Morning Glory can be used as pH indicators because their pigments change colour in acidic or alkaline substances.

Indicators – testing with litmus

Some substances give a particular colour when put in acidic or alkaline solutions. We can use these as indicators to help us decide whether a solution is made from an acid or a soluble base.

Litmus is an example of an indicator. It turns red in acidic solutions and blue in alkaline solutions. You can use litmus solution or litmus paper to test whether solutions are acidic or alkaline.

Using the pH scale

If chemicals dissolve in water, we can test the solution formed with Universal Indicator (UI) paper or solution. This is a mixture of indictors that can be a range of colours depending on the acidity or alkalinity of a solution. The colour is matched to a pH value on the pH scale, which ranges from pH 0 to 14.

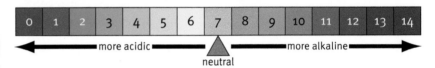

Figure 2.17a The pH scale

- Acids have a pH value below 7.
  The lower the number, the more acidic the solution is.
- Alkalis have a pH value above 7 (an alkali is a base that is soluble in water).
  The higher the number, the more alkaline the solution is.
- A solution with a pH value of 7 is called neutral. Salts made from the reaction between strong acids and strong bases, such as hydrochloric acid and sodium hydroxide, are neutral.

Activity

Distinguishing acids and bases

Your teacher will give you several solutions to test with litmus.

- Make a table to show your results and which solutions are acidic and which are alkaline.

universal indicator solution

0		very acidic
1	hydrochloric acid	
2	lemon juice	
3	orange juice vinegar	
4		
5	black coffee	slightly acidic
6	rainwater	
7	pure water	neutral
8	baking soda	slightly alkaline
9	milk of magnesia soap	
10		
11		
12	washing soda	
13	oven cleaner	very alkaline
14	sodium hydroxide	

Figure 2.17b Some common substances and their pH values. The lower the pH value the more acidic the solution. The higher the pH value the more alkaline the solution. What do we call a solution that is neither acidic nor alkaline?

Activity

Finding out pH values

In this experiment you will test the pH of different solutions using Universal Indictor.

You can either:

● add a few drops of UI solution from a dropping pipette to a small volume of the liquid being tested in a test tube

or

● add a few drops of the liquid being tested to a small piece of UI paper.

Then match the colour against the pH scale.

Record your results in a table like the one below:

Substance tested	Colour of UI	pH value	Acidic, alkaline or neutral?

Did you know?

Hydrochloric acid in your stomach has a pH value of between 2 and 3. Slimy mucus lines the wall of your stomach to protect it from attack by the acid, preventing ulcers.

Key points

● We can measure how strongly acidic or alkaline a solution is using Universal Indicator and the pH scale.

● A pH value less than 7 is acidic.

● A pH value more than 7 is alkaline.

● A pH value 7 is neutral.

Summary questions

1 What colour is litmus in:

   a acid

   b alkali.

2 Why does Universal Indicator give us more information than litmus when testing a solution?

3 Draw the pH scale from 0 to 14, labelling the parts that show 'strongly acidic', 'strongly alkaline', 'weakly acidic', 'weakly alkaline' and 'neutral'.

4 A student collects four solutions in test tubes, but forgets to label them. Solution A has a pH value of 7, solution B is 4, solution C is 14 and solution D has a pH of 1. Match A to D with the following: **vinegar, hydrochloric acid, sodium hydroxide solution, salt solution**.

2.18 Neutralisation

Acids plus bases

Acids and bases (or alkalis) react to make a salt and water. The reaction is called neutralisation. We can show this in a word equation. For example:

hydrochloric   +   sodium ⟶ sodium   +   water
   acid   hydroxide   chloride

acid   **+ base (alkali)** ⟶ **a salt**   **+ water**

In this reaction, if just the right amount of acid and alkali are added together, a neutral solution of the salt sodium chloride is formed.

Activity

Following a neutralisation reaction

Collect 5 cm³ of sodium hydroxide solution in a small flask. Add 5 drops of universal indicator solution.

● What colour is the solution? What is its pH?

Measure out 4 cm³ of dilute hydrochloric acid in a measuring cylinder. Add it to the alkali in the flask.

You can also use a burette to add the acid.

● What colour is the solution now?

As you can see, the solution is still strongly alkaline. You will need to add the next hydrochloric acid a drop at a time. Use a dropper or a burette. Swirl the flask as you add each drop of acid. Try to get a *neutral solution*.

● What colour are you aiming for?

If you add too much acid, you don't have to start again.

● What can you add, a drop at a time, to neutralise the acid?

Uses of neutralisation

We can use neutralisation reactions to remove stains. For example, if fruit juice is spilt on a shirt you can add bicarbonate of soda to remove the stain. The fruit juice is weakly acidic and the bicarbonate of soda is weakly alkaline. Therefore, neutralisation takes place when they are mixed. Borax is another alkaline substance that can be used to neutralise acidic stains, such as tea or wine stains.

Did you know?

The leaf of a nettle is covered in very fine hairs. These are like tiny, sharp, hollow spikes. When you brush against a nettle, the tip of the hair breaks off and the sting from the base of the spike shoots under your skin.

Neutralisation is used to treat acidic insect bites by adding sodium bicarbonate solution, as well as using lime (calcium hydroxide) to raise the pH of acidic soil. It is also used to treat heartburn and indigestion caused by excess acid in your stomach. Indigestion tablets all contain a base to neutralise the acid.

Activity

Which indigestion tablet is best?

You will be given several different indigestion remedies to test.

As a group, decide on a question you would like to investigate.

- Plan your investigation, remembering to make it a fair test.
- Try out some of your ideas to help you plan how much acid and antacid you will use, and how you will measure the effects.
- Record your question, method, results and conclusion.
- Discuss your investigation with other groups. Then evaluate your method, comparing it with those used by other groups.
- Summarise the findings of your class and evaluate the effectiveness of the different remedies.

Key points

- If mixed in the right proportions:

acid + alkali → a neutral solution

- In a neutralisation reaction:

acid + base → a salt + water

- Uses of neutralisation reactions include:
  - raising the pH of acidic soil using lime
  - treating insect stings
  - indigestion remedies.

Summary questions

1 Copy and complete:

When we add an acid to an alkali the pH of the solution goes _____.

When the right amount of acid and alkali _____ together, we get a _____ solution formed, with a pH value of _____. We call this a _____ reaction.

2 When an acid and an alkali react together, a substance called a salt forms. A salt is a solid substance made of crystals.

a Why do you think that you did NOT see a salt forming in your neutralisation experiments?

b How could you get a sample of a salt from the neutral solution formed?

2.19 School–Based Assessment

Your teacher will give you two investigations to tackle and will assess them using the mark scheme shown (see below each Activity box).

The key skills to be assessed are Measurement and Manipulation (MM) and Planning and Design (PD).

Activity (a)

Investigating unknown substances

Your teacher will give you three unknown substances, one acidic, one basic and one neutral.

Your task is to test the pH of the three substances and classify correctly.

- Remember to carry out your pH testing as carefully and as safely as possible.

Practical activity	Manipulation and Measurement	(Maximum 10 marks)
(i) Safety for self and others (2 marks)		
– Demonstrates safety to self and others at all times	2 marks	
– Demonstrates safety to self and others sometimes	1 mark	
– Demonstrates safety to self and others rarely	0 marks	
(ii) Appropriate instrument used (2 marks)		
– Appropriate instrument used always	2 marks	
– Appropriate instrument used sometimes	1 mark	
– Appropriate instrument used rarely	0 marks	
(iii) Accuracy of readings (3 marks)		
– Readings always accurate	3 marks	
– Readings mostly accurate	2 marks	
– Readings rarely accurate	1 mark	
– Readings never accurate	0 marks	
(iv) Competence in use of materials (3 marks)		
– Competent in the use of materials always	3 marks	
– Competent in the use of materials usually	2 marks	
– Competent in the use of materials rarely	1 mark	
– Competent in the use of materials never	0 marks	

Activity (b)

Investigating water

The problem

A student found an unlabelled bottle of a transparent, odourless liquid in the kitchen. The student believes that this liquid is water.

Your task is to design an experiment to determine if this substance is pure water.

- Before you carryout your tests, write down your hypothesis.
- Plan the experiment to find out if the liquid is water or not.
- Explain whether your experiment will prove for sure that the liquid is water or not.

Planning and Design activity	Planning and Design	(Maximum 10 marks)
(i) Hypothesis (2 marks)		
– Testability of hypothesis is clear	2 marks	
– Testability of hypothesis is unclear	1 mark	
– Testability of hypothesis is not possible	0 marks	
(ii) Appropriate method (5 marks)		
– Appropriate methods used always to test hypothesis	5 marks	
– Appropriate methods used mostly to test hypothesis	3–4 marks	
– Appropriate methods used rarely to test hypothesis	1–2 marks	
– Inappropriate methods used to test hypothesis	0 marks	
(iii) Control present (2 marks)		
– Relevant controls stated	2 marks	
– Some controls stated are not relevant	1 mark	
– Controls either not stated or not relevant	0 marks	
(iv) Limitation(s) of the experiment (1 mark)		
– Limitations present	1 mark	
– No limitations	0 marks	

End of module 2 questions

1 a Imagine you and your classmates are the particles in a solid. How would you be arranged in the classroom? Describe any movement you would make.

b How would your movement in the solid change if you imagine that the temperature rises?

c What happens to you and your classmates when the solid melts?

d How would you all pretend to be a gas?

2 This question will help you to remember the chemical symbols of some common elements.

Give the names of the missing elements in the correct order.

Once upon a time, as I floated away light as (He) _____. I saw something as valuable as (Au) _____, but it was even rarer like (Pt) _____. I picked it up and found it was as heavy as (Pb) _____. It reacted easily with water like (K) _____ and (Na) _____ and brightened the place like (Ne) _____ in bulbs. I looked around and saw a piece of (Zn) _____ from a roof, half-buried in the (Si) _____ of the sand.

As I used the (Fe) _____ spade to unearth the piece, I started gasping due to lack of (O) _____ , and realised that a gas cloud of (Cl) _____had been accidentally released from the nearby water treatment plant. I moved as quickly as (Hg) _____ in a thermometer, to put as much distance between myself and the cloud as I could, then stopped to have some (Mg) _____ salts to settle my upset stomach. An old woman standing close by shouted that I was lucky to be alive and should guard my health as if it was valuable like (Ag) _____ is regarded. I thanked her and climbed out of the valley on cables of (Cu) _____ to see labourers applying 'whitewash' containing (Ca) _____ to the fences and around the trunks of the trees, as Christmas would soon be here.

Unfortunately, I fell and bruised my knee and so had to put (I) _____ on the wound to prevent infection. Nearby, a huge industrial complex was releasing toxic clouds containing (S) _____ dioxide and my eyes began to blur and my throat constrict. I began falling as the vehicles whizzing by released the (C) _____ dioxide in their exhaust. I woke up out of the dream I was having.

I then brushed my teeth with the toothpaste containing (F) _____ and went to my bed as it was late at night.

3 Look at the boxes opposite:

Which box shows:

a a mixture of gases

b a solid

c a gas that is a compound

d a pure gas that is made up of only single atoms

e a gas that could be nitrogen gas, N_2?

4 The table below shows the conditions some plants prefer:

Plant	pH range
Apple	5.0–6.5
Potato	4.5–6.0
Blackcurrant	6.0–8.0
Onion	6.0–7.0
Strawberry	5.0–7.0

   a Which plants grow well over the largest *range* of pH values?

   b Which plant can grow in the most acidic soil?

   c Which plant can grow in the most alkaline soil?

   d Describe how you can test the pH of a soil.

   e How can you raise the pH of an acidic soil?

5 The table below shows the pH values of five solutions whose labels have been lost.

Solution	pH value
A	6.0
B	7.5
C	7.0
D	4.5
E	8.0

   a Which solutions are acidic?

   b Soap solution is weakly alkaline. Which of the solutions could be soap solution?

   c i   Give two solutions that would react together.

      ii What do we call this type of reaction?

      iii Two new substances are made in the reaction. One is a salt – what is the other substance formed?

6 Grace was investigating which of four indigestion tablets was most effective. She crushed each tablet and added it to 25 cm^3 of water and an indicator.

Then she added dilute hydrochloric acid 1 cm^3 at a time, until the indicator changed colour.

Here are her results:

Fizzo – 18 cm^3, Neutratabs – 17 cm^3, Soothers – 9 cm^3, Alkomix – 12 cm^3.

   a Put her results in a suitable table.

   b What type of graph would you use to show Grace's results?

   c Which tablet was the most effective?

3 Understanding life
3.1 Living or non-living?

Biology is the study of living things; but what are the features that make living things different from non-living things?

Activity

Living v non-living things

Think of one type of organism that is definitely a living thing, such as a cat.

Think of something that is definitely not a living thing, for example a car.

Make a list of differences between a living thing and a non-living thing.

Figure 3.1a What characteristics make the cat a living thing and the car a non-living thing?

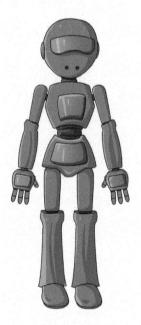

Figure 3.1b Now consider a model robot and a palm tree – explain why one is living and other is non-living.

Figure 3.1c MRS GREN can help us remember the characteristics of living things

Remember this

You can remember the common characteristics of living things by thinking of 'MRS GREN'. These are the first letters of seven essential processes:

- M = Movement
- R = Respiration
- S = Sensitivity
- G = Growth
- R = Reproduction
- E = Excretion
- N = Nutrition

- We all know what **movement** is. It is the ability to change position or travel over some distance. However, some of the other characteristics of living things are less obvious.

- **Respiration** is a process in which living things release the energy they need from food that they eat or in the case of plants, food that they make themselves. (See page 92.)

- **Sensitivity** is the ability to respond to changes in the surroundings. An example is when an animal shivers because it is cold. Another example is when a plant grows towards the light.

- All living things have periods when they grow. **Growth** is a permanent increase in size due to an increase in the number of cells.

- **Reproduction** is the process of making the next generation of living things.

- **Excretion** involves getting rid of waste products, including those made in the cells, from an organism.

- **Nutrition** is the food a living thing takes in to provide essential elements and energy.

In order to carry out these essential processes, living things have an organized structure, made up of a cell or cells.

Key points

- Living things are able to:
  - move
  - respire
  - respond to changes around them
  - grow
  - reproduce
  - excrete
  - feed (take in nutrients).
- Non-livings things cannot perform all of the activities listed above.

Summary questions

1 Make a list of the characteristics of all living things.

2 Look back to the activity box on the previous page.

  Now you know about MRS GREN, explain why a car is classified as a non-living thing.

3 Find out why scientists find it difficult to decide if a virus is a living thing or a non-living thing.

3.2 Comparing animals and plants

Learning outcomes

At the end of this topic you should be able to:

▸ list the differences between animals and plants

▸ classify organisms as animals or plants.

Activity

School grounds survey

Carry out a quick survey of the school's grounds looking at the variety of living things.

● Record your observations. Take photos or video of the specimens.

● Discuss the differences between plants and animals.

● Classify the living things as animals or plants.

● Try to classify the organisms further by deciding if they are vertebrates, invertebrates, flowering plants, or non-flowering plants.

● Use the internet to research the differences between the groups of living things.

To make the study of living things easier, scientists like to classify them. They divide them into smaller groups of organisms such as animals and plants. Animals are further sub-divided into invertebrates and vertebrates, while plants are either non-flowering or flowering (see the flow chart below).

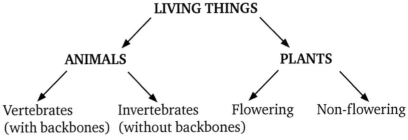

Figure 3.2a Classifying living things

Figure 3.2b Barnacles are sea animals that have evolved to stay still and spend their mature lives in one place, usually on a rock. Once their larvae find a suitable spot to live, they attach themselves permanently. Barnacles are examples of invertebrates as they have no backbone.

How plants differ from animals

● Plants are special because they are capable of making their own food. They can convert substances in their environment to sugar that they can use for energy. The substances that they use to make the sugar are carbon dioxide and water. Energy from the sun is utilized to power the process. This process is called **photosynthesis**. (See page 80.)

● Although plants can move, they do not actually move from one place to another. Animals need to move to find food and mates as well as to escape danger.

- In general, plants take a lot longer than animals to respond to changes in their surroundings. An example is seen in the way shoots grow towards the light. We need time lapse photography to see the movement taking place.

Figure 3.2c Shoots of plants move and grow towards light slowly.

Comparison of animals and plants

Animals	Plants
Cannot make their own food	Make their own food (green and have leaves)
Can move from one place to another/entire organism moves	Plants cannot move from one place to another/parts of the organism move
Generally respond speedily to stimuli	Generally respond slowly to stimuli

Summary questions

1 Describe how plants differ from animals.

2 Name a plant that can respond quickly to stimuli.

3 a Why do animals need to move around, but plants can stay in one place?

   b Name an animal that does not move around, but stays in one place all of its mature life.

71

3.3 Cells

Learning outcomes

At the end of this topic you should be able to:

▸ explain what a cell is

▸ draw the main parts of a cell

▸ describe the functions of the main parts of a cell

▸ state the differences between animal cells and plant cells.

All living things are made up of cells. They are the basic unit of all life on Earth.

Most of these tiny cells are too small to see just using your eyes. You need a microscope to see the structure of cells.

Animal cells

There are many different types of cells in animals but they all share some common features. This is a diagram of a typical animal cell:

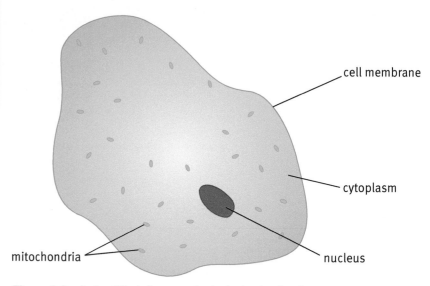

Figure 3.3a A simplified diagram of a typical animal cell

Functions of the cell parts

Each part of a cell has its own particular functions. The parts are all important to make sure a cell works properly.

Cell membrane – This is the outer layer of the cell. It lets simple substances pass into or out of the cell.

Nucleus – This is the 'control centre' of the cell. It controls all the activities in the cell.

Cytoplasm – This is the jelly-like liquid inside the cell. Most of the chemical reactions we need to keep us alive happen in this solution. For example, our cells get the energy they need from respiration, which takes place here.

Mitochondria – These are found in the cytoplasm. They are the sites where respiration takes place and energy is released from our food. These are the energy factories of the cell.

Activity

Making a model cell

Using everyday items and materials design and make a model to represent a typical animal cell.

Explain which parts of your model cell worked as they do in an actual cell and which did not.

Plant cells

Plant cells have the same parts as animal cells but also contain additional features. Here is a diagram of a typical plant cell:

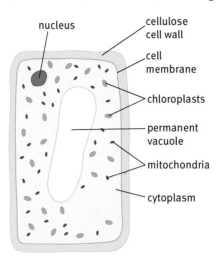

Figure 3.3b A simplified diagram of a typical plant cell

Parts found only in plant cells

Every plant has cells with cell walls.

Cell walls – surround the cell contents (together with their cell membrane) with a rigid boundary. This gives the cell support and shape.

Many plants cells also have:

Chloroplasts – These are the green structures in plant cells where photosynthesis takes place. Photosynthesis is the process by which plants make food.

A **vacuole** – The large central part of the plant cell which is full of cell sap (liquid). This helps to support the plant structure and stores substances.

Summary questions

1 Draw a labelled diagram of:
   a an animal cell
   b a plant cell.

2 What are the differences between a typical plant cell and animal cell?

3 What are the functions of the following parts of a cell:
   a the nucleus   b mitochondria
   c the cell membrane d chloroplasts?

3.4 Specialised cells

The typical animal and plant cells shown previously look different to many of the real cells found in organisms. Many cells have structures that help them to carry out their particular job. They usually have the same basic parts as the typical cells, but look very different.

Below are some examples of animal cells, followed by some plant cells.

Specialised animal cells

Red blood cells

Function – Your red blood cells carry oxygen all around your body.

Special features – The shape of the cell gives it a large surface area to make it better at picking up oxygen from the lungs. The cytoplasm also contains haemoglobin to which oxygen attaches. The red blood cell releases oxygen when it reaches any part of the body requiring oxygen.

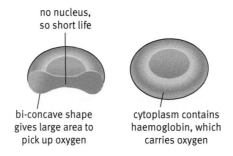

no nucleus, so short life

bi-concave shape gives large area to pick up oxygen

cytoplasm contains haemoglobin, which carries oxygen

Figure 3.4a A red blood cell

Nerve cells

Function – Nerve cells help to transfer messages around the body. The messages are carried as electrical impulses.

Special features – They have long projections to transfer electrical impulses quickly and efficiently. They also have lots of branches at the ends of the cells to make connections to many other nerve cells.

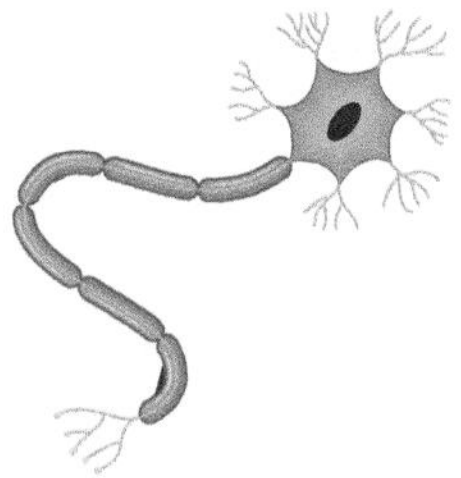

Figure 3.4b A nerve cell

Sperm cells

Function – Sperm cells deliver the male genetic information to the female egg cell (ovum).

Special features – The tail enables the sperm cell to propel itself through fluid to the egg cell. Once it arrives, the 'head' of the sperm cell contains chemicals that help it to break through the outer layer of the egg cell and penetrate the ovum.

Figure 3.4c A sperm cell

Specialised plant cells

Xylem cells

Function – Xylem vessel cells are found in the stems of plants. They carry water and minerals to the leaves and growing parts of the plant.

Special features – The cells are like long tubes, open at both ends, like pipes. This allows water to move up the plant. The sides are made of a tough material that supports the plant. They are made of dead cells.

Guard cells

Function – Guard cells control the flow of gases, including water vapour, in and out of the plant's leaves.

Special features – They work in pairs with a gap between them (called stomata). One side of each cell is thicker than the other. When they fill with water, the cells bend into a banana-like shape, opening up the stomata. This allows gases to escape from the leaf. In dry conditions the cells lie flat and close the stomata so water vapour cannot escape to the atmosphere.

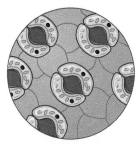

open stomata

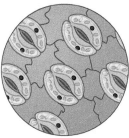

closed stomata

Figure 3.4d Guard cells in action

Activity

Research a specialised cell

Carry out some research to find out about another specialised animal cell and plant cell.

Examples could be:

- Animal cell – an egg cell, epithelial cell
- Plant cell – root hair cell, phloem cell

Create a booklet, fact book, e-book or poster to share this information with the general public.

Display your findings for the rest of your class.

Key points

- Specialised cells are adapted to carry out their particular functions. They have features that are not found in typical plant and animal cells.

- Examples include sperm cells and red blood cells in animals, and xylem cells and guard cells in plants.

Summary questions

1 What do we mean by a 'specialised cell'?

2 In a table list the functions and special features of two specialised animal cells and two specialised plant cells.

3.5 Organised organisms

Learning outcomes

At the end of this topic you should be able to:

▸ illustrate the levels of organisation of an organism using a flow chart

▸ state the major animal and plant systems

▸ name some of the main organs in an organism's system.

Did you know?

There are more than 200 different types of cell in your body.

We have seen how cells are the essential building blocks of living things. Many organisms are made up of lots of different types of cells that work together in groups.

Groups of similar cells working together form **tissues**. Examples include muscle tissue, nerve tissue and connective tissue.

Different types of tissue combine to form **organs**. Examples of organs in animals include the heart, kidneys and liver, and plant organs include the root, stem and leaves.

Organs also work together in groups to carry out life processes, such as reproduction. These are called **organ systems**. They include the circulatory system and the respiratory system.

The organ systems make up the complete organism, such as a dog or a palm tree.

To summarise:

cells ➠ tissues ➠ organs ➠ organ systems ➠ whole organism

Here are the organ systems that enable organisms to stay alive:

System	Function	Some major organs
Digestive	Breaks down food	Mouth, gullet, stomach, intestines
Excretory	Eliminates wastes	Kidneys, bladder Leaves, stems
Nervous	Coordinates responses	Brain, spinal cord, sense organs
Reproductive	Produces offspring	Testes, uterus, ovary, penis Flowers
Skeletal	Provides support Enables movement	Limbs Xylem
Transport	Enables movement of substances	Heart, blood vessels Stem, root
Respiratory	Enables exchange of gases	Lungs Leaves

Organs and organ systems

Choose one organ system from either an animal or a plant.

Find out more information about your chosen organ system. Give more detail than that included in the table on the opposite page about its functions and the organs involved.

Prepare a presentation to share with the rest of your class.

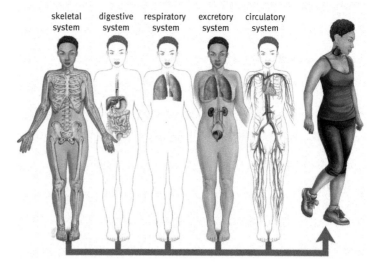

skeletal system digestive system respiratory system excretory system circulatory system

Figure 3.5a Some of the organ systems that make up the human body

Key points

- Complex living organisms are organised in the following way:
  cells ➡ tissues ➡ organs ➡ organ systems ➡ whole organism

- Organ systems include the reproductive, nervous, respiratory, circulatory, skeletal, transport and digestive systems.

Summary questions

1 Draw a flow chart showing how a complete organism can be broken down to its basic units, the cells.

2 Which organ in the body:

   a pumps blood around

   b gets rid of waste and regulates water

   c takes in and gives out gases to and from the blood?

3 What is the main function of:

   a the nervous system

   b the digestive system

   c the excretory system?

3.6 Plants: the producers

Learning outcomes

At the end of this topic you should be able to:

▸ define the terms 'producer', 'consumer', 'food chain' and 'food web'

▸ draw a simple food chain

▸ explain how the organisms in a food web affect each other.

Food chains

All the energy for life on Earth comes from the sun.

This energy is passed from organism to organism along **food chains**. A food chain shows the energy flow as the different organisms feed on each other.

Each food chain will start with a green plant or algae. This is because these organisms are able to 'capture' the sun's energy.

Plants or algae use the sun's energy to photosynthesise. Photosynthesis is the process by which plants make their food. A sugar called glucose is made (see page 80).

The plant or algae at the start of a food chain is called a **producer**.

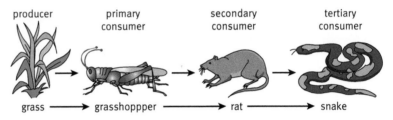

Figure 3.6a A simple food chain

- In Figure 3.6a the producer is grass.
- A **herbivore** (plant-eater), in this case a grasshopper, eats the grass. The grasshopper is the primary **consumer** in the food chain.
- Then the grasshopper is eaten by a rat, the secondary consumer. Rats are examples of omnivores because they will eat animals or plants.
- The rat is then eaten by the snake, the tertiary consumer in this food chain. The snake is a **carnivore** (meat-eater).
- Energy from each organism is passed along the chain in the direction of the arrows.

This is a terrestrial food chain as it takes place on land. Food chains are also found in aquatic environments such as seas, rivers, creeks and ponds. For example, this is a food chain from a lake:

algae ⇢ water snail ⇢ crayfish ⇢ crane

Remember this

Food chains always start with a plant (or algae) and the arrows point away towards the consumers.

Food webs

In nature, food chains do not exist by themselves. Animals seldom eat just one type of organism. In order to survive they eat a variety of plants and/or animals. The overlapping of food chains produces a food web.

Look at Figure 3.6b.

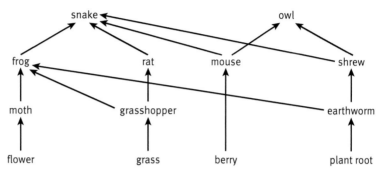

Figure 3.6b An example of a simplified food web

- Any large changes in the numbers of a species in the food web will affect the other species. For example, if a pesticide kills many of the grasshoppers, then the number of rats could be decreased.
- Decreasing the rats will mean one of the food sources of the snake is affected. They might need to eat more mice and shrews which will affect the food stocks of the owls.
- With fewer shrews the earthworm population could rise.

Key points

- Feeding relationships in a particular habitat can be described by food chains.
- Food chains overlap to form food webs.
- Energy flows along the food chain.
- Changes in the numbers of a species in a food chain or food web affect the other species.

Summary questions

1 Here is a food chain:

    grass ➡ cow ➡ man

    a Name the consumers in the food chain.

    b Give an example of a carnivore and a herbivore from the food chain.

    c Name the producer in the food chain.

    d Describe the flow of energy in the food chain.

2 If a disease wiped out the population of snakes in the food chain in Question 1, what would happen to the number of:

    a rats

    b frogs

    c moths?

3.7 Photosynthesis

Learning outcomes

At the end of this topic you should be able to:

▶ label a diagram of a leaf

▶ state the word equation for photosynthesis

▶ identify the raw materials and products of photosynthesis.

On the previous spread we saw that plants can make their own food, so they form the bottom level of food chains. But how do they make their food?

Most food is made in the plant's leaves. The basic structure of a leaf is shown in Figure 3.7a.

● Plants use carbon dioxide from the air and water from the ground for photosynthesis. The raw materials are carbon dioxide (from the air) and water (from the ground).

● In a series of reactions in green parts of a plant, the raw materials (carbon dioxide and water) are turned into glucose (the plant's food) and oxygen gas. Glucose is a sugar.

● Chlorophyll is a green pigment in chloroplasts inside plant cells. The chlorophyll absorbs light energy from the Sun. Photosynthesis needs this energy to take place.

We can summarise photosynthesis by this word equation:

$$\text{carbon dioxide + water} \xrightarrow[\substack{\text{to 'trap' light} \\ \text{energy from the sun}}]{\text{chlorophyll}} \text{glucose + oxygen}$$

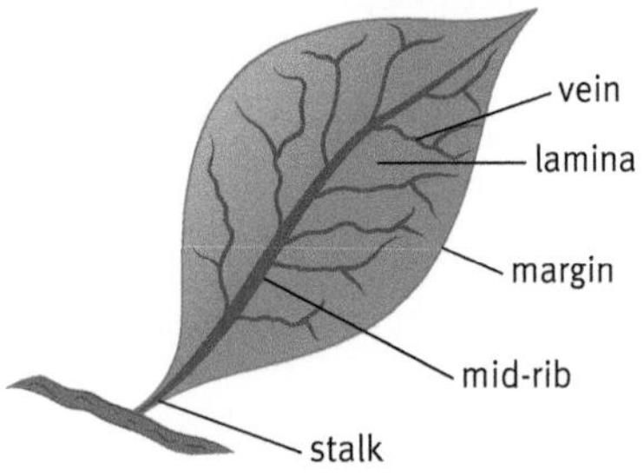

vein

lamina

margin

mid-rib

stalk

Figure 3.7a A simple diagram of a leaf

Remember this

Wherever we find chloroplasts in plants – photosynthesis takes place.

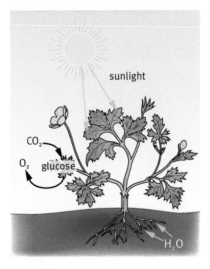

sunlight

CO_2

O_2 glucose

H_2O

Figure 3.7b **Summary of photosynthesis** – carbon dioxide is taken in through the leaves and water is drawn up through the roots. Glucose is made, as well as oxygen gas which is released into the air.

Testing for starch

Much of the glucose made is stored as starch in the plant. If we find glucose or starch in a plant, we know that photosynthesis has taken place. Fortunately there is a quick and easy test for starch.

Iodine solution turns from brown to dark blue/black with starch.

Activity

Are light and chlorophyll needed for photosynthesis?

We can de-starch a plant by leaving it inside a dark cupboard for 24 hours.

Using this fact, and the safety warning below, plan a test on a leaf:

a   to find out if starch is made in a leaf that is kept in the dark

b   to find out if chlorophyll (the green pigment in a leaf) is needed to make starch. You can use a variegated leaf (one which has white patches on it with no chlorophyll) to do this test.

Let your teacher check your plan before you start any practical work.

Safety: Ethanol is a flammable liquid. It catches fire very easily, so the ethanol must be boiled by putting boiling water from a kettle in the larger beaker.

Iodine solution stains skin and clothes. Students should use disposable gloves and lab coats should be worn when performing this experiment.

Figure 3.7c Iodine solution turns dark blue/black in starch.

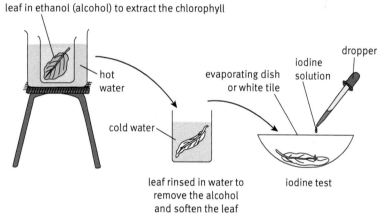

Figure 3.7d Testing a leaf for starch

Key points

- Photosynthesis can be summarised as:

  carbon dioxide + water $\longrightarrow$ glucose + oxygen

- The glucose made can be turned into starch which stores energy in the plant.

Summary questions

1   Draw a labelled diagram of a leaf.

2   Write a word equation to summarise the process of photosynthesis.

3   What is chlorophyll needed for in photosynthesis?

4   Which substance do we use to test for starch? What is the result of a positive test?

5   Explain why we test for starch.

3.8 Flowering plants

Sexual reproduction needs male and female sex cells to meet and fuse together. This type of reproduction takes place in most plants and animals.

Structure of flowers

- Flowers have **both** male and female parts.
- The male organs are called stamen. They make pollen. Pollen grains contain male sex cells.
- The female parts are in the carpel.
- They make the female sex cells called ova (egg cells) inside an ovule.

Look at Figure 3.8a:

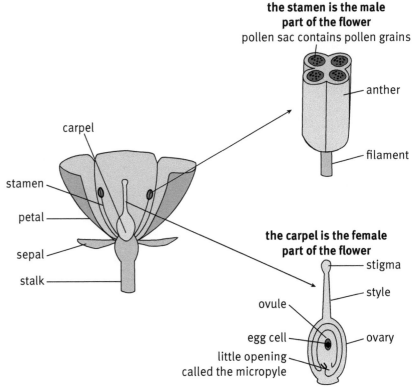

the stamen is the male part of the flower
pollen sac contains pollen grains
anther
filament

carpel
stamen
petal
sepal
stalk

the carpel is the female part of the flower
stigma
style
ovule
egg cell
ovary
little opening called the micropyle

Figure 3.8a The structure of a flower

Function of the parts of a flower

Male parts of a flower

The stamen is made up of the anther and filament.

The filament is the thin stalk, on top of which the anther is found. The anther produces pollen grains.

Female parts of a flower

A carpel is made up of the stigma, style, and ovary. Some flowers contain many carpels at their centre. The word 'pistil' is used to describe the female parts of a flower whether it contains a single carpel or many carpels.

The male and female sex cells meet and fuse together in the carpel (pistil), making seeds. In many instances the carpel matures and forms the fruit around the seeds.

Other parts of a flower

Petals protect the reproductive parts of the flowering plant. They are often coloured in order to attract insects and other pollinators.

Sepals are found around the base of the petals. They protect the young flower (bud).

The stalk connects the flowering part of the plant to the rest of the plant.

Activity

Identifying the parts of a flowering plant

Using a flower with a single carpel, attempt to identify the parts of the flower described on this page.

Key points

- In flowering plants, the male parts are called the stamen and the female part is the pistil. The pistil may contain one or many carpels).
- The flower's main function is to produce new plants.

Summary questions

1 Draw a large diagram of a section through a flower (a flower that has been sliced in half, top to bottom). Label the diagram and include the function of each part of the flower.

2 Which two parts of flower make up the stamen?

3 How does a leaf of a flowering plant differ from its petals?

3.9 Pollination

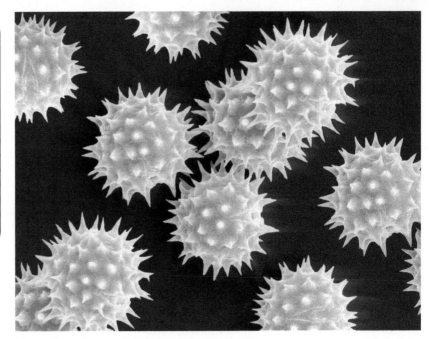

Figure 3.9a A magnified image of pollen grains

In sexual reproduction in a flowering plant, the male sex cells in the pollen must meet the female sex cell inside the ovule. The pollen is transferred in a process called **pollination**. In pollination, the pollen lands on the sticky stigma at the top of the carpel.

The pollen can get to the stigma of another plant of the same species in three ways.

Animal pollination

In plants, with brightly coloured petals, the pollen is most likely to be transferred by insects. Insects, such as bees, are attracted by the colours. They feed on the sweet-smelling, sugary nectar inside the centre of the flower. As insects feed, pollen sticks to their legs. When the insect moves to a neighbouring flower to feed on more nectar, the pollen is transferred to its stigma. Pollen can also be transferred between flowers by birds and bats.

Figure 3.9b This plant is pollinated by insects transporting pollen from one plant to another plant of the same species

Wind pollination

Other flowering plants, such as grasses, do not need insects for pollination to takev place. They grow long, feathery stamen with lots of light pollen grains. Their pollen grains can be blown to the stigmas of other flowering plants by the wind.

Water pollination

Aquatic flowering plants can release their pollen into the water in which they grow. Then water currents move the pollen onto other plants, just like the wind does on land.

Self-pollination and cross-pollination

The agents of pollination we have looked at (animals, wind and water) carry pollen from one plant to another. If the pollen is from a plant of the same species as the plant it lands upon, pollination can take place. We call this cross-pollination because two plants are involved.

However, some plants can pollinate themselves. The pollen transfers directly from the anthers of a flower to the stigma of the **same** flower (or another flower on the same plant). This is self-pollination. Only one plant is involved.

Figure 3.9c This grass is wind pollinated

Key points

- Pollen is carried from stamen to the stigma by animals, wind or water.
- Self-pollination involves just one plant but cross-pollination involves two plants (of the same species).

Summary questions

1 Copy and complete:

   During the process of _____, pollen grains are transferred from the _____ to the _____ of a flower. _____ grains can be transferred to other flowering plants by _____, _____ or _____.

2 What is the difference between self-pollination and cross-pollination?

3 Look at the pollen grains in Figure 3.9a. Describe their appearance. Give reasons for the appearance.

3.10 Fertilisation and seeds

Pollination

Once the pollen has lands on the stigma, the male sex cell, has to reach the egg cell inside the ovule.

● The pollen grain grows a tube down the style into the ovary.

● The male gamete passes down the tube and on into an ovule.

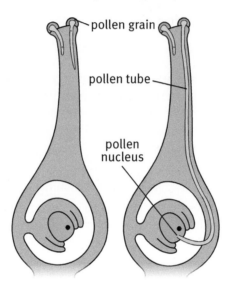

Figure 3.10a The pollen tube grows down from the pollen grain on the stigma to the ovary

Fertilisation

The male and female gametes join together as fertilisation takes place.

● The fertilized cell produces a seed and the ovary matures into a fruit. Think of a tomato – you can see the seeds embedded inside the fleshy fruit that was once the ovary in a tomato plant.

Germination

Germination is the process whereby the baby plant within a seed begins to develop into a new plant. A seed is a food store, which the new plant uses to grow and develop. Eventually it will grow its own leaves. The young plant can then begin to photosynthesise and make its own food.

To germinate, the seed needs:

● energy

● oxygen

● a suitable temperature

● water.

Activity

Investigating germination

Plan and carry out an investigation to find out how either

- temperature,
- water, or
- air

affects the germination of seeds.

Write up your investigation, as shown in Module 1.

Remember that you can be assessed on your 'Recording and Communicating' and 'Analysis and Interpretation' skills in this investigation.

in order for a new plant to develop.

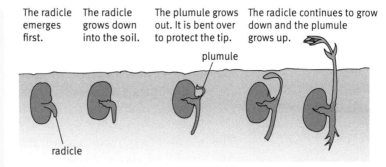

The radicle emerges first.

The radicle grows down into the soil.

The plumule grows out. It is bent over to protect the tip.

The radicle continues to grow down and the plumule grows up.

plumule

radicle

Figure 3.10b The germination and early growth of a plant

During germination the radicle (root) bursts through the micropyle (tiny hole in the seed coat) and begins to grow downwards into the soil. Next, a plumule (shoot) begins to grow upwards towards the light. The shoot produces green leaves so the plant can begin the process of photosynthesis. Oxygen is obtained from the air and used for respiration.

Temperature is important – if it is too high or too low, germination will not take place. Water in the soil helps the coat (testa) of the seed to soften and makes it easier for the radicle and plumule to grow out of the seed.

Key points

- The male sex cell joins with the female sex cell in an ovule within the ovary via a pollen tube which grows down the style.
- Sexual reproduction in plants involves a male sex cell and a female sex cell fusing together when fertilisation takes place.
- Germinating seeds need energy, oxygen, warmth, and water in order to produce a new plant.

Summary questions

1 Draw a flow diagram to explain sexual reproduction in a flowering plant.

2 Draw a flow diagram to describe how a seed produces a young plant.

3 What conditions are needed for a seed to germinate?

3.11 Gases in the air

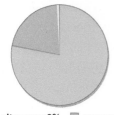

☐ nitrogen 78% ☐ oxygen 21%
☐ argon (an inert gas) 0.9%
☐ carbon dioxide 0.04%
☐ trace amounts of other gases (including other inert gases)

Figure 3.11a The relative proportions of nitrogen, oxygen and other gases in the Earth's atmosphere

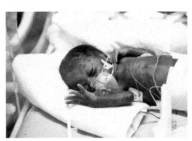

Figure 3.11b Premature babies are helped to breathe using oxygen gas

Plants and animals need gases from the air to survive. Oxygen and carbon dioxide are important gases for living things. Oxygen is needed for respiration and carbon dioxide is needed for photosynthesis. However, there are also other gases in our atmosphere. Look at the pie chart in Figure 3.11a.

The percentage of water vapour in the air differs from place to place and from day to day around the world. It is referred to as the humidity – the more water vapour in the air, the more humid is the weather.

Uses of nitrogen

Nitrogen gas is very unreactive so people use it in sealed food packaging to stop food from spoiling. It is also used on oil tankers when the oil is pumped ashore to reduce the risk of explosion.

In industry, nitrogen gas is used to make ammonia. This is then converted into **fertilisers**.

Liquid nitrogen (boiling point –196°C) is used to cool things down to very low temperatures. At these temperatures most things solidify. It is used to store sperm in hospitals to help in fertility treatment.

Uses of oxygen

Oxygen is the reactive gas in the air. Whenever fuels burn, they are reacting with oxygen gas. It is also used to help substances react. Examples include high temperature welding and in the steel making process.

Oxygen is used to help people breathe, often at the scene of an accident or in hospital. Mountaineers use oxygen in breathing apparatus on high altitude climbs. Oxygen is needed for respiration in most living things.

Uses of carbon dioxide

Carbon dioxide is essential for plant life as it is needed for photosynthesis.

If carbon dioxide is cooled down to about –45°C, it solidifies. As a solid it is used as a refrigerant to keep things cold, and as dry ice used for 'misty' stage effects. Carbon dioxide is also dissolved under pressure into carbonated (fizzy) drinks.

Carbon dioxide does not support combustion, so it is used in fire extinguishers (see Figure 3.11c). These are especially useful on electrical fires where water might make the situation worse.

Figure 3.11c Carbon dioxide gas smothers a fire, starving it of oxygen

Figure 3.11e Argon (unlike oxygen) does not react with the white hot tungsten metal in this type of light bulb

Uses of inert gases

The word 'inert' means unreactive. The inert gases are listed in the periodic table (see page 46 in the last column).

Neon gas is used for red lighting in advertising.

Helium gas is used to inflate balloons and 'blimps' seen at big sporting events.

Figure 3.11d Helium gas has a very low density and is safe to use in airships

Argon gas is used inside incandescent light bulbs. This stops the white hot metal filament from reacting with oxygen and snapping.

School-Based Assessment

Your teacher can assess your presentation for the skills of 'Recording and Communicating' and 'Social attributes'.

Activity

More about gases

Work as a small group with each person choosing one of the gases from atmosphere. Individually research and find more detailed information about the uses of your chosen gas. Combine your group's findings into a 'Uses of gases in the air' presentation.

Choose an interesting method to present your findings to the rest of the class.

Key points

- The main gas in the atmosphere is nitrogen, making up 78%.
- Oxygen is the reactive gas in the atmosphere. It makes up 21% of the air.
- Small amounts of other gases, such as carbon dioxide, argon, neon and water vapour, are also present in the atmosphere.

Summary questions

1 Draw a table to show the gases present in the air and their approximate proportions.
2 Which gas in the atmosphere is:
  a needed for combustion
  b used inside incandescent light bulbs
  c is used to make fertilisers in industry?

3.12 Investigating inhaled and exhaled air

Learning outcome

At the end of this topic you should be able to:

▸ compare the air we breathe in with the air we breathe out.

The air we breathe in (inhaled air) is different from the air we breathe out (exhaled air).

You can carry out the following tests to compare inhaled and exhaled air.

Activity

Testing for carbon dioxide

Set up the apparatus shown to test whether inhaled or exhaled air contains more than carbon dioxide.

The limewater will turn cloudy more quickly in the tube which has more carbon dioxide gas passing through it.

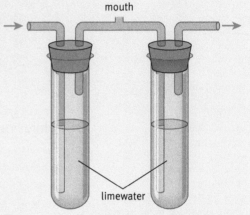

Figure 3.12a Testing inhaled and exhaled air for carbon dioxide gas

Activity

Other tests comparing inhaled and exhaled air

a Time how long it takes for a candle flame to go out under a beaker of air and under a beaker of exhaled air.

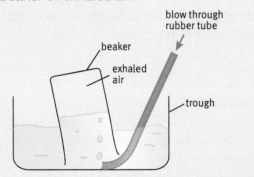

Figure 3.12b Collecting a beaker of exhaled air

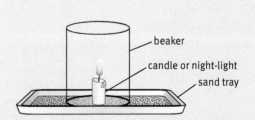

Figure 3.12c Burning a candle in exhaled air

What do you find?

b Measure the temperature of the air.

Then breathe out onto the bulb of the thermometer for a minute and take the temperature again.

What do you find?

c 1. Breathe out onto a mirror

2. Move the mirror through air.

What do you observe in EACH case?

Record your results of a, b and c in a table.

• Experiment a shows us that inhaled air contains more oxygen than exhaled air. For example, a candle, in which wax is reacting with oxygen, will burn longer in a beaker of normal air compared with a beaker of exhaled air.

Key points

	Inhaled air	Exhaled air
Carbon dioxide	Less	More
Oxygen	More	Less
Warmth	Less	More
Moisture	Less	More

Summary questions

1 How do we test for carbon dioxide gas? What is the positive result of this test?

2 Describe the differences between inhaled and exhaled air.

3 a What is percentage of nitrogen gas in inhaled air?

b What happens to the percentage of nitrogen in exhaled air compared to inhaled air?

4 a Draw a 2D scientific diagram of the apparatus used to test whether inhaled or exhaled air contains more carbon dioxide gas.

b Explain in detail how this experiment works as you breathe in and out of the mouthpiece.

3.13 Respiration

Learning outcomes

At the end of this topic you should be able to:

▶ state the word equation for respiration

▶ explain the importance of respiration for living things.

Just think of all the activities you do in a day. They all need energy. Some are obvious, such as riding a bike or running. Every time we use a muscle, energy is required.

- We need energy every time our heart beats and every time we breathe in and out.

- Energy is required for all the reactions and processes that cells need to function. It is essential for their metabolism.

So where do we get the energy to sustain life?

Respiration is the process by which the cells in living things obtain their energy.

Figure 3.13a The energy we need to run, as well as all other activities, comes from the process of respiration

- Cells release some of the chemical energy stored in carbohydrate molecules in their mitochondria.

- Respiration is not really achieved in a single chemical reaction. A complex series of reactions takes place in our cells. However, we can summarise respiration by the following equation:

glucose + oxygen $\longrightarrow$ carbon dioxide + water (+ ENERGY)
    (raw materials)   (products)

Remember this

The raw materials for respiration are glucose and oxygen. The products are carbon dioxide and water. We do not call 'energy' a product as it is not a substance.

Taking in the raw materials

Our bodies need to get the raw materials needed for respiration from our surroundings.

- Glucose comes from some of the foods we take in. Carbohydrates are known as good sources of energy because we can break them down into glucose. This happens as we digest our food.
- The glucose passes through our intestines into the bloodstream. It can then be carried in the blood to the cells.
- The oxygen needed for respiration is taken in when we inhale. On page 91 it was stated that the air we breathe out contains less oxygen than the air we breathe in.
- Some of the oxygen taken into our lungs passes into our blood.
- The oxygen dissolved in blood is carried to cells by haemoglobin in our red blood cells.

Getting rid of the waste products

Carbon dioxide and water are waste products that are made during respiration. They are removed from the body when we breathe out. They pass from our blood into the lungs, and then out into air.

Note that not all of the water made in respiration is removed from the body via exhalation.

Remember this

Remember that the equation for respiration is the reverse of the equation for photosynthesis.

Key points

- Respiration releases all the energy required for life processes.
- Respiration uses oxygen to release energy from glucose.
- Carbon dioxide and water are made as the waste products of respiration.

Summary questions

1 Copy and complete:

   Organisms need _____ for all life processes. This is provided during the process of _____.

   The raw materials are _____ and _____.

   The products are _____ and _____. _____ is released in the process.

2 Write the word equation to represent respiration.

3 Explain where we get the raw materials needed for respiration and how we get rid of the waste products from our bodies.

3.14 Air pollution

Did you know?

After a smoker finishes a cigarette, up to 10% of their blood will be carrying carbon monoxide, so is not available to carry oxygen.

Activity

Air pollution – research

Working as part of a group, choose one of the air pollutants covered here and find out some more information.

Present your findings to the rest of your class.

The increase in the number of industries and cars on the roads has resulted in air pollution becoming a major problem.

Causes of air pollution

Carbon dioxide

- The main compounds in fossil fuels are made of hydrogen and carbon (hydrocarbons). Fossil fuels are used to run vehicles, produce electricity and power machinery in factories. These fuels burn in a good supply of air to form carbon dioxide and water:
  hydrocarbon + oxygen $\longrightarrow$ carbon dioxide + water
- Carbon dioxide levels in the atmosphere have rapidly increased over the last century.

Its effects

Carbon dioxide is called a greenhouse gas. It absorbs energy given off from the Earth as it cools down and traps it close to the surface of the Earth. The average temperature of the Earth has been rising, mainly because of the increase in the amount of carbon dioxide in the atmosphere. This is called global warming. People are worried that global warming will cause rising sea levels and flooding in low-lying land. It could also affect climates around the world and cause more extreme weather events, such as storms, hurricanes and droughts.

Sulphur dioxide

- Whenever we burn a fossil fuel, there is also a chance that sulphur dioxide gas will be given off. The sulphur is one of the impurities in fossil fuels.
- The metal extraction industry also produces sulphur dioxide gas which can be released into the atmosphere.

Its effects

Sulphur dioxide causes breathing problems. It makes asthma worse as it irritates the lining of the lungs. Sulphur dioxide also causes acid rain which affects forests and lakes, together with the plants and animals that live there. It also attacks and corrodes buildings, especially those made of limestone, and metal structures.

Carbon monoxide

- Carbon monoxide is a toxic gas. It is made when fuels burn in insufficient oxygen.

Figure 3.14a Carbon monoxide is produced by car engines. Modern cars have catalytic converters fitted in their exhaust system to remove most of this toxic gas. However, they change carbon monoxide to carbon dioxide, which is still an air pollutant.

School-Based Assessment

Your teacher can look at your presentation to assess your skills in 'Recoding and Communicating' and 'Social attributes'.

Key points

- Air pollution is caused by carbon dioxide, carbon monoxide, sulphur dioxide, methane and particulates released by human activity.

- Carbon dioxide and methane are greenhouse gases which cause global warming. Sulphur dioxide causes acid rain.

- Air pollutants can cause various lung diseases, such as asthma, allergies and lung cancer.

- If there is not enough oxygen, some of the carbon in the fuel turns into carbon monoxide instead of carbon dioxide. This happens inside car engines.

Its effect

Carbon monoxide is colourless and odourless so you do not realise when you are breathing it in. This makes the toxic gas particularly dangerous.

Particulates

- Particulates are tiny particles in the air, such as those given off from diesel engines.

- Sahara dust and smog are also sources of particles, which can be breathed into the lungs.

Their effect

Particulates irritate the breathing passages in the lungs and could lead to cancers.

Methane

- Methane is released from fields used to grow rice, marshlands and grazing cattle as a waste product.

- As the human population rises, more land is being used for growing rice and raising cattle to feed us all. This causes methane levels in the atmosphere to increase.

Its effect

Methane is another greenhouse gas, like carbon dioxide. It is a more effective absorber of energy than carbon dioxide, but there is not as much of it in the air.

Summary questions

1 Complete a table like the one below:

Air pollutant	Sources	Harmful effects
Carbon dioxide		
Carbon monoxide		
Sulphur dioxide		
Methane		
Particulates		

2 Explain why carbon monoxide is such a dangerous gas.

3.15 Pests and pest control

Did you know?

The mongoose was introduced into some Caribbean islands to kill rats that were gnawing the mature sugar cane plants. The primarily diurnal mongoose did not encounter the primarily nocturnal rats and were therefore a poor choice for biological control. The mongoose has been responsible for dramatically reducing the populations of harmless snakes on these islands.

Plant pests are unwanted organisms that can decrease the expected yield of a crop plant. This results in less food being available for human consumption.

Types of plant pests

(a) Other plants, for example, weeds;

Farmers do not want weeds growing between their crop plants because the weeds take nutrients and water from the soil and take up valuable space. This will result in competition between the crops and the weeds for the available resources for growth. Therfore the crops will not grow to their full potential.

(b) Plant parasites, for example, dodder;

Some plants are parasitic, growing on their host plants. They use the nutrients the host plant absorbs from the soil or makes in photosynthesis. Dodder is an example that attaches itself to other plants and can entwine a crop. They do not necessarily kill the crop but they affect its growth by 'stealing' the nutrients from the plants themselves.

Figure 3.15a Dodder growing on host plants.

(c) Insects, for example, caterpillar;

Many insects and their larvae are herbivores – they feed on plants. So insects can damage crops as they grow.

(d) Other animals, for example, rats; parasites such as worms.

Animals, such as mice and rats, feed on crop plants, especially the seeds of maize. Therefore they affect the yield of grain. They will also infest grain kept in storage sheds after being harvested.

Parasitic worms can also infect root crops, feeding off the plant's nutrients. For example, tapeworms can get into the roots of crops from infected animal manure used as fertiliser. These can then infect humans if left untreated.

Figure 3.15b Selective herbicides are used to control weeds on agricultural land. They kill the weeds but not the crop plants.

Controlling plant pests

Weeds can be controlled by spraying them with herbicides. However, care must be taken that the chemicals used do not cause harm to the environment or the food chains in the ecosystem. Organic farmers do not use chemicals on their crops. They remove weeds physically by hand, or mechanically – using hand tools or machinery.

Farmers often control insect pests and their larvae with chemicals called insecticides. Rats can be controlled either by chemical means (rat poison) or mechanical means (baited traps).

Pests can also be controlled in agriculture by biological means. The farmer will introduce a predator to feed on the pest. An example is the ladybird which feeds on aphids (a plant pest). Another species introduced on Caribbean islands is the cane toad. This feeds on pests, such as the white-grub that attack the sugar cane crop. They were even introduced into Jamaica to control rats, although this did not seem to work.

Spiders can also be used to decrease the numbers of flies.

Activity

Plant pest – research

Working as part of a group, choose one plant pest and find out some more information.

Present your findings to the rest of your class. Your presentation must include:

- the name of the plant your chosen pest affects
- its impact on the plant
- methods of control
- possible effects of the control methods on the environment.

Key points

- Types of plant pests:
  - other plants, for example, weeds
  - plant parasites, for example, dodder
  - insects, for example, caterpillars
  - other animals, for example, rats; parasites, for example, tapeworms.
- Pests and parasites can be controlled by biological (predatory organisms), chemical (pesticides) or mechanical (barriers or traps) means.

Summary questions

1 Mice are seen as a pest once they infest a farm. Give an example of **a** biological, **b** chemical **c** mechanical method that could be used to control them.

2 Explain where you might find ladybirds used on an organic farm.

3 Why are parasitic worms on root crops dangerous?

4 How can pesticides harm our environment?

3.16 Soils

All soils contain tiny pieces of rock, often formed from the breakdown of the bedrock beneath it.

Types of soil

The characteristics of each type of soil are determined by:

- the size of the rock fragments it contains,
- the chemical composition of the rock fragments, and
- the amount of other organic materials mixed in it. This organic material is called **humus** and originates from living organisms.

Some people classify soils into just three categories:

- clay
- sandy
- loam.

A **clay soil** contains very tiny pieces of weathered rock. This means that there are few gaps between particles for water to drain through. Therefore clay soil can get waterlogged in the rainy season. It contains little air, especially when wet, because there is not much space between its small particles. You can recognise clay soil as it is lumpy and sticky when wet but turns rock-hard and cracks when dried out.

Compare this with a **sandy soil**, which feels gritty to the touch, and drains water quickly because of its larger grains of rock. This also means that there are more gaps between soil particles for air (which is needed by organisms that live in the soil e.g. the roots of plants). The sandy soil does have a disadvantage in that heavy rain can wash away the soluble nutrients from the soil. We say that the nutrients are leached from the soil.

Loam soil has a more equal mixture of small and large grains of rock. So it can retain water without getting waterlogged. It also contains more humus than clay or sandy soil.

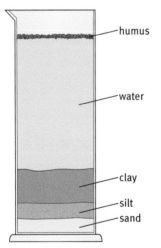

Figure 3.16a Sedimentation test: stir two large spatulas of soil in a measuring cylinder of water then leave it to stand overnight.

Testing the physical properties of soils

Permeability is measured by the rate at which water can drain through a soil (see figure 3.16b).

- The amount of water held in the soil depends not only on its particle size, but also on the percentage of humus. The more humus, the better the soil can retain water for use by plants.
- The humus also provides most of the nutrients that a plant needs. It is made from dead plant material and animal waste, as well as their decomposing bodies. The organic material is broken down into more simple substances. Plants absorb these useful substances, so they are recycled.

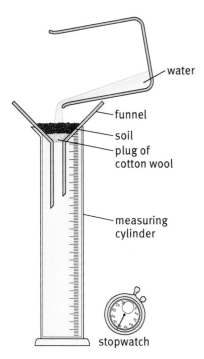

water

funnel

soil

plug of
cotton wool

measuring
cylinder

stopwatch

Figure 3.16b Measuring the
permeability of soil

Activity

Comparing soils

Plan and carry out tests on the three soil types (sandy, clay and loam) to compare the following properties:

- texture (by mixing with water and rolling into a ball),
- particle size,
- water holding capacity,
- drainage
- air content.

Record your investigation as shown in Module 1.

Remember your teacher can assess your skills in 'Recording and Communicating' and 'Analysis and Interpretation' in this soil investigation.

Key points

- There are three types of soil – clay, sandy and loam.
- A soil's physical properties are determined by its particle size as well as water, air and humus content. Loam soil is the most fertile for growing most crops.
- Clay contains the smallest grains and sand the largest; but loam contains a more even mixture of grains (as well as more humus).

Summary questions

1 What is soil made up of?
2 Name the three main types of soil.
3 Draw a table to compare the grain sizes, water retention and amount of air in the three types of soil.
4 Explain why a clay soil becomes waterlogged more easily than other types of soil.

3.17 More about soils

Think of some reasons why soil is so important to us.

- Soil is vitally important because it is the medium in which plants grow, and plants are needed as a food source for living things.
- Plants use the soil to anchor themselves in a stable position.
- Plants also get their nutrients from soluble minerals in the soil. They absorb these dissolved minerals through their roots.

Soil erosion

In certain places, the top-soil (in which plants grow) can be blown away by the **wind** or washed away by **rainwater**.

The soil can be removed in sheets, like a land-slide or in channels (small ones are called rills and deeper ones are called gullies).

This soil erosion is more likely if an area:

- has had all its plants removed by over-grazing, because plant roots bind the soil together
- is on a slope because water will flow down, taking the soil with it.
- is not sheltered as the full force of the wind can cause maximum damage.

Figure 3.17a Soil can be removed by wind or, as in this case, by water

Soil conservation

Farmers can protect their soil from erosion by:

- not removing all plant-life from an area
- creating flatter terraces to grow crops on a sloping site – this is expensive to set up as it requires a lot of labour and large

Activity

Soil erosion and conservation

Find out more about soil erosion and soil conservation. If possible visit some sites and take photos of examples.

Make a presentation to show your findings to the rest of the class.

School-Based Assessment

Your teacher can assess your skills in 'Recording and Communicating' and 'Analysis and Interpretation' in this research and presentation task.

amounts of stone and rock to support the terraces – but it does make farming the flatter land much easier than working on a slope

- planting alternate rows of crops between rows of soil-binding plants, such as grass
- sowing their crops at right angles across the slope of an inclined field – a technique called contour ploughing
- planting hedges or constructing wind-breaks around fields to shelter soil from the wind.

However, severe weather events, such as hurricanes or floods can still quickly erode the soil despite there being precautions in place.

Figure 3.17b Planting crops on terraces helps prevent water rushing down a slope and eroding top-soil away

Key points

- Soil erosion is caused by wind and rainwater.
- Farmers have ways of reducing the loss of top-soil, such as terracing on steep land.

Summary questions

1 What do we mean by soil erosion and why does it take place?
2 List the ways in which farmers can reduce the risk of soil erosion.
3 Why does soil erosion sometimes take place even if farmers have taken measures to stop it?

End of module 3 questions

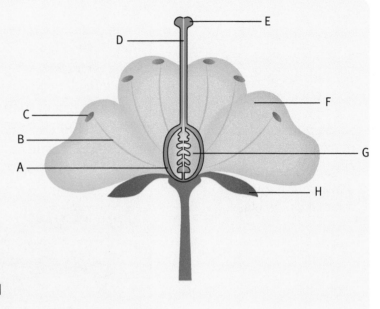

1 Identify the labels A to H on the diagram using the words below:

stalk   ovule   sepal
stigma   filament ovary
anther   petal

2 Which one of the following cell parts contains the green pigment that plants need for photosynthesis?

   A Nucleus   B Cell wall

   C Choroplasts   D Vacuole

3 a i Name the cell parts that we find in both animal cells and plant cells.

     ii What extra cell parts can be found in some plant cells?

   b Which part of a cell:

     i   allows substances to pass in and out of the cell

     ii controls the functions of the cell

     iii is the jelly-like substance in which all the chemical reactions take place?

   c Why are the roots of a plant not green in colour?

4 Many cells in plants and animals are specialised cells.

   Look at the diagram of a cell found in the root of a plant opposite:

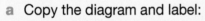

   a Copy the diagram and label:

     i   the nucleus   ii the vacuole   iii the cell wall

   b State one cell part the root cell does not have but a leaf cell does have.

   c Think about the function of a root. How is the cell shown specialised to do its job?

5 Plants make their own food.

   a What do we call the process in which plants make their own food?

   b i Name the two substances that plants take in from their surroundings in order to make their food.

     ii Name the two substances made in this process.

     iii Which substance is used to 'trap' energy from the sun in this process?

   c Two students wanted to find out if changing the intensity of light falling on a water plant affected how quickly the process described above takes place. They used the apparatus drawn at the top of the next page:

Describe how they could carry out their investigation.

6 Farmer Brown's land lies on a slope.

  a Explain which direction Farmer Brown should plough his fields?

  b Farmer Brown lets a neighbour's goats graze on one of his sloping fields over the winter. When he checks his land in spring he finds all the vegetation has been eaten. State two ways that this could affect his soil.

  c i Farmer Brown has one field that is so steep he struggles to use a tractor on it. Suggest what construction work he could do to solve the problem.

    ii What other benefit would Farmer Brown get in this field when his work was finished?

7 This question is about gases in the atmosphere.

  a Which gas makes up most of the atmosphere around us?

  b Which gas in the atmosphere will turn limewater cloudy (milky)?

  c Name the reactive gas in the atmosphere.

  d Which gas is put in incandescent light bulbs? Why?

  e Which gas is used in food packaging to stop food going off?

8 When we burn fossil fuels we pollute our atmosphere.

  a Which two products are made when a fossil fuel burns completely in plenty of air?

  b If there is not enough air present when a fossil fuel burns we can get a toxic gas formed.

    i Name this toxic gas.

    ii Why is this gas so dangerous in a confined space?

  c Impurities in fossil fuels can lead to a gas being given off that causes acid rain. Name this gas.

  d What name do we give to the tiny solid particles released into the air when fuels are burned?

  e Name two gases that could be responsible for global warming.

9 a List four types of pests that can affect plant crops.

  b What environmental damage can be done by using pesticides to control pests in an irresponsible manner?

10 a Describe how the apparatus opposite can be used to compare inhaled and exhaled air.

  b List three differences between inhaled and exhaled air.

  c i Write down the word equation that describes what happens in respiration.

    ii Why is respiration so important for living things?

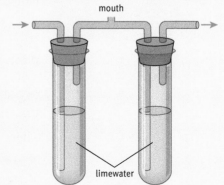

mouth

limewater

4 Focusing on me
4.1 Puberty

Learning outcomes

At the end of this topic you should be able to:

▸ state the approximate age range of puberty

▸ define the term puberty

▸ list the secondary sexual characteristics in males and those in females.

The period during which you change from childhood to adulthood is called adolescence. This is a time of great change in everyone's life.

During adolescence, you will normally have a growth spurt. You start to grow more quickly for a year or two, as well as going through emotional changes.

The first stage of adolescence is called puberty. This is the time when your body changes as you develop **secondary sexual characteristics**.

Puberty usually takes place in girls at about 10 to 13 years of age. In boys the changes often start at about 12 to 14 years of age. However, some people start earlier and some start later.

Activity

Secondary sexual characteristics

Look at Figure 4.1a.

Make a list of differences that arise as a child changes to an adult.

Mark each difference as 'male', 'female' or 'both'.

Figure 4.1a There are differences seen between the mother and her daughter, and the father and his son, because of the development of secondary sexual characteristics

As well as differences we can see, puberty brings differences that cannot be seen. Puberty begins when a child's body starts to produce more **sex hormones**. These chemicals can make puberty a difficult time for young people and their families. They can trigger emotional changes in the young person, which are hard to understand.

These sex hormones are:

- **oestrogen** – which is produced in the ovaries of girls.
- **testosterone** – which is produced in the testes of boys.

Did you know?

An egg (ovum) is released from the ovary once every month in a mature female. Each month the lining of the womb (uterus) thickens. This prepares it to receive a fertilised egg. If an egg is not fertilised then the lining breaks down. It flows out of the body through the vagina. This flow of blood and tissue (the lining of the uterus) is commonly called a "period". A girl's period may last between 3 and 7 days. A period is one of the steps in the female menstrual cycle.

In a male, the testes will start to produce sperm. They will make millions of sperm, ready to fertilise an egg.

Figure 4.1b gives a summary of the changes in the human body that take place in puberty.

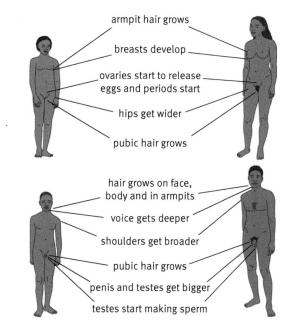

armpit hair grows

breasts develop

ovaries start to release eggs and periods start

hips get wider

pubic hair grows

hair grows on face, body and in armpits

voice gets deeper

shoulders get broader

pubic hair grows

penis and testes get bigger

testes start making sperm

Figure 4.1b Changes at puberty

Key points

- Puberty is the time of change from childhood to adulthood.
- Secondary sexual characteristics of males are voice deepening, more muscle formation and growth of pubic hair.
- Secondary sexual characteristics of females are the development of breasts, widening of the hips and growth of pubic hair.

Summary questions

1 Between which ages does puberty usually take place in:

a girls

b boys.

2 Write down the changes that take place in a boy during puberty.

3 Make a list of changes in a girl that take place in puberty.

4 What causes puberty to start?

4.2 The reproductive system

Figures 4.2a and 4.2b show the reproductive organs of human females and males. They are designed to make new humans. The organs help a sperm (the male sex cell) to meet up and fuse with an ovum or egg (the female sex cell).

The female then needs to provide a safe place for a new baby to develop until it is ready to be born.

Female reproductive system

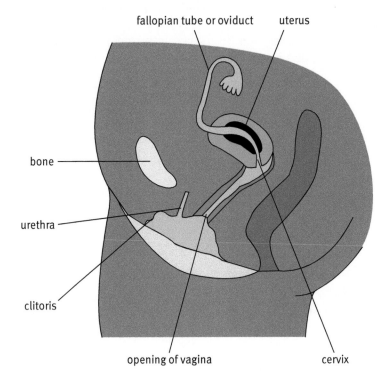

Figure 4.2a The female human reproductive system

Here are the female sex organs and their functions:

● Ovary – production of egg
● Fallopian tube (oviduct) – carries the egg from the ovary towards the uterus.
● Uterus (commonly called the womb) – where the foetus develops into a baby
● Cervix – holds a mucus plug during pregnancy
● Vagina – birth canal through which the baby leaves the mother

Male reproductive system

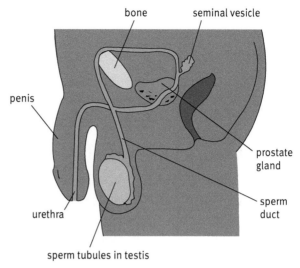

bone

seminal vesicle

penis

prostate gland

urethra

sperm duct

sperm tubules in testis

Figure 4.2b The male human reproductive system

Here are the parts of the male reproductive system and their functions:

- Testes – produce sperm
- Urethra – carries semen and urine to the outside of the male body
- Sperm duct – passage-way for sperm to enter the urethra
- Penis – allows for penetration into the vagina
- Prostate – provides fluids and nutrients to help sperm move around

Activity

The human reproductive system

Your teacher will give you diagrams of the male and female reproductive systems.

Label the diagrams.

Key points

- The male and female reproductive systems produce sex cells.
- The major organs in the male reproductive system are the testes.
- The major organs in the female reproductive system are the ovaries.

Summary questions

1 Draw two tables to show the parts of the male and female reproductive system and their functions.

2 Why do sperm need fluid to function?

3 Give another commonly used word for the uterus.

4.3 Starting a new life

Fertilisation

A new life starts when a sperm meets and fertilises an egg cell (or ovum). This joins together genes from a male and female to make a new individual. This takes place after a man and woman have sexual intercourse (make love) – see Figure 4.3a.

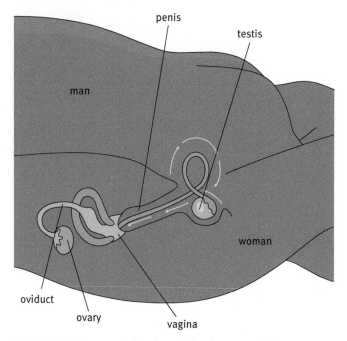

Figure 4.3a Fertilisation can take place following sexual intercourse

When a man makes love, extra blood will flow into his penis. This makes it bigger and it becomes hard. When a woman is ready, her vagina gets wider and makes extra fluid so that the penis can slide in more easily.

Eventually sperm are pumped from the testes. The sperm mix with fluid produced in a number of glands. The sperm and fluids mix to make a secretion called **semen**. Semen is pumped into the vagina. This is called ejaculation and is usually accompanied by orgasm.

Once the sperm are in the vagina, they start to swim towards the uterus.

Did you know?

Out of around 300 million sperms that enter the vagina during sexual intercourse, about 1 million get through the cervix and enter the uterus.

If an egg has recently been released from an ovary, one sperm might break through the outer layer of the egg. The sperm nucleus enters the egg and joins with the nucleus of the egg. This is called fertilisation.

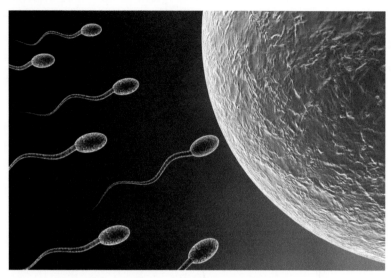

Figure 4.3b Sperm around an egg – usually only one sperm can actually break through and enter the egg

Once an egg has been fertilised it carries genetic information from both the mother and father. It continues to move down the oviduct. It divides into 2 cells, then 4, then 8 cells, then 16 cells and so on until it is a ball of cells. It is now called an embryo.

Did you know?

Sperm can live for about four days in the fallopian tubes – so if an egg is released in this time it can be fertilised.

An egg can survive for about three days after its release from the ovary. It is able to be fertilised if it is penetrated by a sperm during this time.

Key points

The male sex cell and female sex cell meet and fuse together in fertilisation.

A sperm penetrates an egg cell and the sex cells join to start the process of making a new human.

Once fertilised the cell divides and forms an embryo.

Summary questions

1 What do we mean by 'fertilisation' in human reproduction?

2 a What is the male sex cell called?

   b What is the female sex cell called?

3 What is an embryo?

   Include how a fertilised egg turns into an embryo in your answer.

4.4 Pregnancy

Once a female has an egg fertilised, we say that she is pregnant.

- Pregnancy is the time between fertilisation and birth. This period of time in humans usually lasts for 39 weeks or 9 months.
- During pregnancy, the fertilised egg travels down the fallopian tube to the uterus. It then implants itself into the lining of the uterus.
- The embryo grows there, attached to the mother via the placenta and umbilical cord. The embryo develops into a foetus. The foetus is protected in the uterus by a bag of amniotic fluid. The fluid cushions the foetus.

The mother's blood provides nutrients to the blood of the embryo or foetus. That is why it is important for a mother to eat a good diet during pregnancy. She must also avoid smoking, drugs and alcohol. Harmful substances in the mother's blood will pass into the blood of the foetus, and can cause damage to the growing foetus.

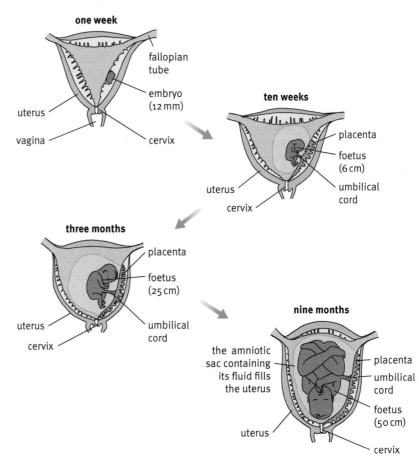

Figure 4.4a The stages of pregnancy

The stages of labour and birth

Labour is the process of giving birth to the baby. It happens about 9 months after fertilisation and is usually completed in about 24 hours.

First stage of labour

- During the first stage of labour the muscles of the uterus start to contract. This is caused by the release of a hormone in the mother's body.
- This hormone may also cause the membrane around the baby to break releasing the amniotic fluid. This is when we say 'the mother's water has broken'.
- The cervix becomes thinner and widens or dilates.

Second stage of labour

- The second stage of labour begins when the cervix is fully dilated. The midwife can follow the progress of the labour by feeling the width of the gap in the cervix.
- When the cervix is wide enough, the baby passes through, usually head first, and is delivered from the vagina.

Third stage of labour

- The third stage involves the placenta separating from the wall of the uterus and being delivered as the afterbirth.
- Once the placenta is delivered, the umbilical cord is clamped and cut, and the baby given to the mother.

Did you know?

The baby passes through the cervix when the opening is about 10 cm wide.

Did you know?

Doctor's can sample the amniotic fluid to check for genetic abnormalities in the foetus.

Activity

From fertilisation to birth

Draw a flow chart to show the sequence of events from fertilisation to the birth of a baby.

Alternatively show the above by giving a presentation with visual aids to the rest of your class.

Key points

- The embryo implants itself into the wall of the uterus.
- The embryo develops into a foetus in the uterus during pregnancy.
- The embryo/foetus can get its food and oxygen from the mother's blood through the placenta.
- About 9 months after fertilisation, the mother goes into labour and the baby is born.

Summary questions

1 How does the foetus receive its nutrients during pregnancy?

2 How is the foetus protected in the uterus?

3 What happens during the third stage of labour?

4.5 Pre- and post-natal care

Learning outcome

At the end of this topic you should be able to:

▸ explain the need for pre-natal and post-natal care in humans.

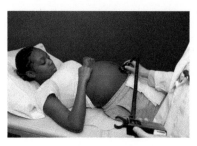

Figure 4.5a It is important to monitor the progress of the mother and foetus in pregnancy, and this continues after the birth of the baby

Pre-natal care

Pre-natal care monitors a woman's health during pregnancy. It also deals with the health and development of her unborn baby. Pre-natal care can help predict any possible problems with the pregnancy or birth. As a result, actions can be taken to avoid or treat any issues identified.

Smoking, alcohol and drugs

Harmful substances in tobacco smoke, alcohol and drugs can be passed from the mother's blood across the placenta to the baby. Health workers in clinics will warn pregnant women of the dangers.

Smoking is one of the most damaging factors to the health of the unborn baby. Risks include miscarriage, stillbirth, low birth weight babies that fail to thrive and higher risks of foetal abnormalities.

Alcohol is a poison. It can damage both the sperm and egg, as well as the developing embryo. The main risks to the baby are mental retardation, retarded growth, and damage to the brain and nervous system.

Both prescribed and recreational drugs can cause harm. Marijuana interferes with normal production of male sperm and the effects take 3 to 9 months to wear off. Hard drugs such as cocaine, heroin and morphine can damage the chromosomes in the sperm and ovum. This can lead to abnormalities in the embryo.

Diet

It is important that the mother has a balanced diet during pregnancy (see page 128). This ensures that the baby will get all the nutrients it needs for growth and development.

Diseases in pregnancy

Disease can pass from the mother to the foetus in her uterus. German measles (rubella) is caused by a virus that can cross the placenta. It causes abnormalities, such as deafness and heart defects. Sexually transmitted diseases (STIs) can damage the foetus in the uterus or the baby as it is born. So health professionals can check for these at the first visit to the clinic (and later in the pregnancy for women at risk). The HIV virus that causes AIDS may cross the placenta. Therefore a baby may be born HIV positive if the mother is infected with the virus.

Scanning during pregnancy

X-rays are high energy waves. They are harmful to the developing foetus. Therefore we cannot use them to scan development of the foetus. Instead hospitals use ultrasound. This is a safer, less energetic wave than X-rays. A scan checks to find out if the unborn baby is healthy, using the image produced on a monitor.

Post-natal care

Following the birth, mothers take their new baby to a clinic to monitor their progress.

Immunisation of the baby

During the first year of life, babies are immunised (vaccinated) against certain dangerous diseases. These could cause death or lasting damage. Examples are:

- measles, mumps and rubella (MMR),
- whooping cough, diphtheria, tetanus, polio.

Figure 4.5b It is important that babies are immunised against certain diseases

Activity

Healthy mothers and babies

Your task is to produce a health leaflet for pregnant women explaining the benefits of pre- and post-natal care.

Find out:

- why breast-milk is necessary for the development of the new-born baby
- why some mothers choose to feed their babies on formula milk.

Key points

- Pre-natal care looks after the needs of mothers and their unborn babies during pregnancy.
- Post-natal care monitors the mother and baby following the birth during the baby's first year of life.

Summary questions

1 Make a list of diseases against which babies can be immunised.

2 Besides diseases, make a list of other factors that can harm the unborn baby.

3 Explain the difference between pre-natal care and post-natal care.

4.6 Contraception

Learning outcomes

At the end of this topic you should be able to:

▸ list the major types of contraception

▸ describe briefly the basic principles behind different methods of contraception

▸ discuss the impact of teenage pregnancy.

Birth control (or family planning) allows you to plan when and how many children you want. If two people want to have sexual intercourse without a sperm fertilising an ovum then they need to use contraception.

Some people think it is wrong to make love just for pleasure, so they do not believe in using contraception. They will not have sexual intercourse unless they want a child. We say that they **abstain** from sex at other times.

There are different methods of contraception. Some are shown in the following table.

Natural methods

Method	Description	Advantages	Disadvantages
Withdrawal	Penis is withdrawn from vagina before ejaculation.	No side effects.	Fluid released before ejaculation may contain sperm. No protection against STIs. Unreliable.
Rhythm methods	More mucus is produced and there is a rise in body temperature when eggs are released. So intercourse is avoided for a few days before and after this time.	No side effects. Recommended by Catholic church. Can be used to plan a pregnancy. No chemicals or physical products used.	Not very reliable as the time when an egg is released can be difficult to predict. Need to abstain from sex at fertile times or use a condom or another method. It takes three or four menstrual cycles to learn effectively when the eggs are being released. You should keep daily records.

Barrier methods

Method	Description	Advantages	Disadvantages
Male condom	Made from very thin rubber; it is put over the erect penis and stops sperm from entering the vagina.	No medical side effects. Easy to obtain free from some clinics and sold widely. Can help protect both partners from some STIs, including HIV.	Putting it on can interrupt sexual intercourse. May slip off or split if not used properly. May reduce sensitivity of penis.
Female condom	A soft, thin polyurethane sheath loosely lines the vagina. It covers the area just outside and stops sperm from entering the vagina.	Can be put in any time before sexual intercourse. Can help protect both partners from some STIs, including HIV. No medical side effects.	Putting it in can interrupt sexual intercourse. May be difficult to use. May get pushed into the vagina. Not as widely available as the male condom.
Diaphragm/ cap with chemical spermicide	A flexible rubber dome-shaped device, used with spermicide, is put into the vagina to cover the cervix. This stops sperm from entering the uterus and meeting an egg.	Can be put in at any time before sexual intercourse. No serious health risks. Gives some protection against STIs.	Putting it in can interrupt sexual intercourse. More reliable if used with spermicide, but some people can be sensitive to spermicide. Correct size needs to be known. It needs replacing if a woman changes weight, i.e. gain or loss of more than 3 kg. May be damaged during intercourse.
Intra-uterine device (IUD)	A small plastic and copper device which is put into the uterus by a doctor. It stops the sperm reaching an egg or stops a fertilised egg implanting in the uterus.	Works as soon as it is put in. Can stay in for five to ten years but can be taken out at any time. Once removed fertility will return to normal.	No protection against sexually transmitted diseases. Periods may be heavier or more painful. Can cause infection of the uterus.

Continued

Hormonal methods

Method	Description	Advantages	Disadvantages
Contraceptive pill (also available as patch, injection or implant)	It contains hormones that can: – thickens cervical mucus to prevent sperm reaching the egg, – prevent implantation, – prevent egg release.	Simple to take: one tablet a day; patch changed weekly; injection lasts for 12 weeks.	No protection against sexually transmitted diseases. May have temporary side effects. Increased risk of heart disease and high blood pressure. Not reliable if vomiting and diarrhoea occurs after taking or on course of antibiotics.

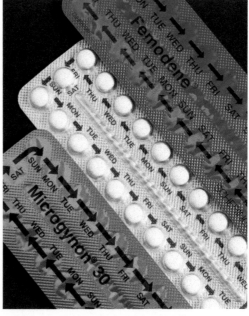

Figure 4.6a A packet of contraceptive pills – the days of the week are labelled on the packaging to remind women to take them each day

Surgical methods

Method	Female sterilization (tubal ligation)	Male sterilization (vasectomy)
Description	The fallopian tubes are cut, sealed or blocked by an operation. This stops the egg and sperm meeting.	The tubes (ducts) that carry sperm from the testicles are cut, sealed or blocked.
Advantages	Sterilization is permanent. No long or short term serious side effects. No need to think about contraception.	Permanent with no side effects. No need to think about contraception.
Disadvantages	Not often reversible. No protection from STIs or HIV	Usually permanent so can't be reversed (although the tubes can be repaired in rare cases). Some people think it might increase the risk of testicular cancer.

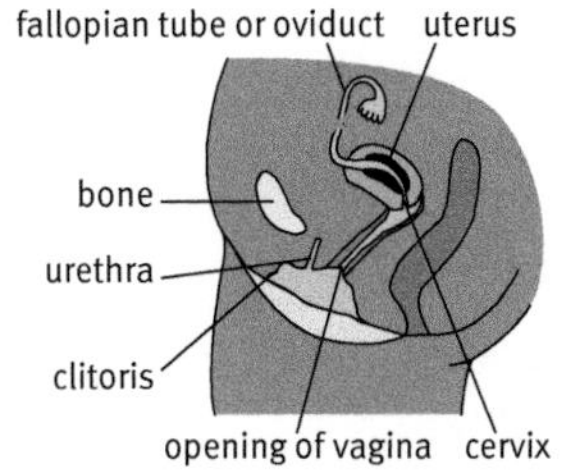

Figure 4.6b Both of the Fallopian tubes from the left and right ovaries need to be cut, sealed or blocked.

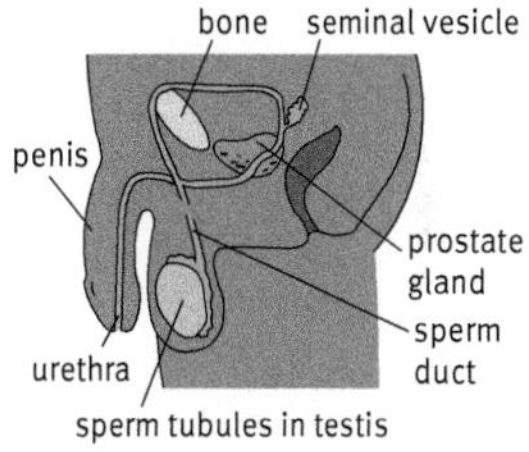

Figure 4.6c Both of the sperm ducts from each testicle need to be cut, sealed or blocked in a surgical procedure called a vascectomy.

Summary questions

1 Match each method of contraception to a relevant statement:

Method of contraception	How it works/examples
Abstinence	prevents egg release
Barrier methods	no sexual activity
Chemical spermicide	examples are rhythm and withdrawal methods
Contraceptive pill	surgical prevention, for example, vasectomy, tubal ligation
Natural	kills sperms
Sterilisation	condoms, diaphragm, IUD

2 Which method of contraception:

a depends on a woman's ability to predict her monthly ovulation?

b relies on "tricking" the female body with chemicals?

c prevents sperm from entering the vagina and protects against sexually transmitted infections?

4.7 Reproductive health checks

Learning outcome

At the end of this topic you should be able to:

▸ discuss the importance of screening for health problems associated with the reproductive organs.

The most obvious diseases of the reproductive organs are sexually transmitted infections (STI's). These are passed from one person to another during sexual activity.

An STI can be caused by viruses, bacteria, or parasites, such as fungus.

- Some infections are caused by bacteria, such as chlamydia, gonorrhea and syphilis. These are usually curable.
- However, infections caused by viruses such as HPV, genital herpes, hepatitis B and HIV cannot be cured.

Any of the symptoms below should be checked out immediately by a doctor.

Bacterial infections

STI	Symptoms of disease caused	Treatment
Chlamydia	Women often show no signs. Lower abdominal back pain; nausea; fever.	Treated by antibiotics – if left untreated, it can cause infertility.
Gonorrhoea	First symptoms appear between 2 to 7 days after infection in a woman, but most women show no signs. Some have thick cloudy or bloody vaginal discharge and frequent urination. Men have thick yellow-green discharge from penis; sores develop on the penis and pain on urinating.	Treated with antibiotics, although some strains are resistant.
Syphilis	Painless sores on the genitals that can last 3 to 6 weeks then disappear; swollen glands; skin rashes.	Curable with antibiotics; but if left untreated can lead to blindness and paralysis.

Activity

Viral infections

Do some research to fill in the table below:

STI	Symptoms of disease caused	Treatment	Should we screen for this disease?
Human papilloma virus (HPV)			
Genital herpes			
Hepatitis B			
Human immunodeficiency virus (HIV)			

Did you know?

Figures reported in 2011 indicate that the Caribbean has the highest age-standardised mortality rate from prostate cancer in the world, and it is by far the most common cancer found in Jamaican men.

Activity

Screening for cancers of reproductive organs

Choose one of the following diseases and carry out some research on it:

- breast cancer   • prostate cancer   • cervical cancer.

Write a short newspaper article on why we should screen for these cancers.

Key points

- Sexually transmitted infections are passed between partners having unprotected sex.
- Bacterial infections are treated with antibiotics, but there is no cure for viral infections to date.
- Abstinence or using a condom protects against STI's.

Summary questions

1 Draw a table with two headings to show examples of bacterial and viral STI's.

2 Why would somebody who ignored their symptoms of syphilis mistakenly think their problem had been solved after a couple of months? Why would this be a very serious mistake?

3 Name one organ in the male and one in the female reproductive systems that cause many deaths each year because they become cancerous.

4.8 Drugs

What are drugs?

Drugs are substances that affect the normal way the body functions. These include medical drugs and recreational drugs.

Medical drugs affect the body to help cure it of disease or relieve its symptoms. Aspirin, paracetamol and penicillin are examples of medical drugs.

Recreational drugs have no long lasting benefits for the body. They often affect the brain or your nervous system. They can make people feel good but can be addictive.

Addicts of a drug cannot live without it. They get to depend on it. If they try to stop they get withdrawal symptoms. These make the addict feel ill and ache, with an over-powering craving for their drug.

Some recreational drugs are legal and some are illegal. Look at the table:

Legal recreational drugs	Illegal recreational drugs
alcohol	marijuana or cannabis
nicotine (in cigarette smoke)	cocaine
caffeine (in coffee, tea, cola)	heroin
	amphetamines, such as ecstasy

Legal drugs

Legal drugs, such as nicotine and caffeine act as stimulants in the body. They make the heart beat faster and raise blood pressure. You probably know some people who need a cigarette (providing nicotine) or a cup of coffee (providing caffeine) to 'get them going' in the morning. They also use the nicotine or caffeine to keep awake when working long hours.

However, cigarettes can seriously damage your health, as the warning indicates on the packet!

Cigarette smoke contains thousands of chemicals, some of which cause cancer. There is a strong link between smoking and lung cancer, and other diseases of the lungs. The tar in the smoke sticks in the lungs and gives smokers their frequent cough. It also causes cancer. Smoker's high blood pressure also causes heart disease. It increases the risk of heart attacks and strokes.

Figure 4.8a Despite the health warning, it is difficult to quit smoking once you start as nicotine is an addictive drug

Remember this

Both legal and illegal drugs can become additive to users. Some people get addicted to prescription, drugs, such as pain-killers or sleeping pills.

A little alcohol tends to relax people. This drug slows down your heart rate and reflexes. That is why drinking alcohol and driving is so dangerous. Alcoholics are addicted to alcohol. Drinking heavily damages the liver and causes many deaths of young people every year.

Illegal drugs

Marijuana (or cannabis) slows down your brain activity. Other illegal drugs, such as cocaine and amphetamines make you more alert. However, drugs like cocaine are extremely addictive. Drugs can become an expensive habit. Some people turn to crime to fund their addiction. Their personal lives fall apart as the drug becomes the most important thing in their lives.

Hard drugs damage your body and addicts often lead poor lifestyles.

Activity

The life of a drug addict

Write a short story about a day in the life of a teenager, drug addict who has fallen on hard times.

Key points

- Drugs affect the workings of the body in some way.
- There are medical drugs and recreational drugs.
- Some recreational drugs are legal but others are illegal.

Summary questions

1 Name three medical drugs.
2 Name two legal recreational drugs and two illegal recreational drugs.
3 What are the effects of smoking cigarettes on your health?
4 Why do people addicted to drugs find it difficult to stop taking them?

4.9 Diseases

The human body can be affected by different types of diseases. We can classify these diseases into four groups:

- nutritional deficiency diseases
- physiological diseases
- inherited disorders
- infectious diseases.

Nutritional deficiency diseases

'Nutritional deficiency' means a shortage in one or more of the essential nutrients that the body needs to function. If this shortage lasts a while, then it can lead to a nutritional deficiency disease.

A lack of vitamin C in the diet leads to scurvy. Other examples of nutritional deficiency diseases are anaemia, goitre, and rickets.

Anaemia

If you have anaemia, you may have too few red blood cells or too little haemoglobin in your red blood cells. This can be caused by a lack of iron, vitamin B12 or folic acid in your diet. However, there are other causes.

Red blood cells carry oxygen around the body, so if there is a problem with them you do not get enough oxygen to your cells. This can make you feel tired or get breathless easily. Many people are cured by taking iron or vitamin supplements.

Goitre

People with goitre have a lump in the neck as a result of a swelling in their thyroid gland. This is caused by a lack of iodine in the diet. We get iodine from seafood, such as fish, shellfish or seaweed, from cereals or grains, and from cow's milk.

Rickets

Rickets is a softening of the bones due to a lack of vitamin D. We can get vitamin D from foods, like oily fish and eggs or from sunshine.

Physiological diseases

Physiological diseases involve cells, tissue or organs failing to function properly. There are many of these diseases, with diabetes and cancer being two of the most serious.

Diabetes

Diabetes is a condition in which glucose builds up in the blood. Insulin is produced in the pancreas to help glucose get into your

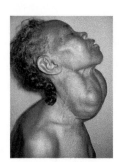

Figure 4.9a Goitre is caused by a lack of iodine in the diet

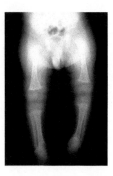

Figure 4.9b Rickets can be caused by a lack of vitamin D

cells. There it is used to release energy (in respiration). There are two types of diabetes – Type 1, in which no insulin is made, and Type 2, in which not enough insulin is made or it does not work properly. Both types of diabetes are treated by leading a healthy lifestyle, but Type 1 also requires daily insulin injections.

Cancers

Cancer is caused by abnormal cells that start to divide without control. The cancer cells can spread to other tissues around the body through the blood and lymph system.

Inherited disorders

Some conditions are passed on through families by defective genes.

Sickle cell anaemia

Sickle cell anaemia is a disorder passed down through families in which red blood cells are crescent-shaped.

As explained on the previous page, problems with red blood cells mean that body cells can be starved of oxygen. The condition can result in episodes of pain throughout the body and managing these is an important part of treatments.

Haemophilia

People with haemophilia have inherited a disorder that means they have difficulty clotting blood when they are cut or when blood vessels break. So they have to take great care to avoid injuries. They can be treated with drugs or artificial clotting factor.

Infectious diseases

Infectious diseases are mainly caused by bacteria, viruses, parasites or fungi. They can be spread easily from person to person. There are many common examples, such as influenza, sexually transmitted infections, dengue fever and ringworm.

Summary questions

1 Draw a table showing the different types of diseases, their causes, and give two examples of each.

2 Give two reasons why people can be anaemic.

3 Explain what causes the two types of diabetes.

4 Find out what causes the following infectious diseases and how they are passed from person to person:

   a influenza   **b** dengue fever   **c** gonorrhoea.

4.10 Lifestyle choices

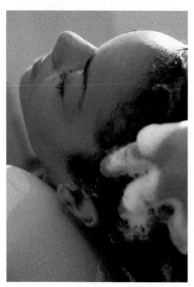

Figure 4.10a Clean hair is an essential part of good personal hygiene

Your body's natural smells become stronger at puberty and personal hygiene becomes more important. Nobody likes to get too close to someone with a very strong personal odour. So when you reach puberty, you have to ensure high standards of personal hygiene.

Just as important is the need to keep clean to prevent disease. The bacteria that cause disease thrive in dirty conditions.

Did you know?

Your body has nearly two million sweat glands. They release sweat to cool down the body when necessary.

Personal hygiene

The points below need to be followed to ensure your personal hygiene:

Regular washing of the hair

Small insects called headlice can breed undisturbed in dirty hair. Head lice are easily spread from one person to another by contact. Dirty hair can also cause dryness and itchiness of the scalp, which is one cause of dandruff.

Care of teeth

You should brush your teeth at least twice a day. If not, bits of food can get stuck in the gaps between your teeth. This encourages the growth of bacteria which feed on sugars to produce acid. The acid causes tooth decay. The bacteria also cause plaque to build up on teeth. This can lead to bad breath and gum disease.

Regular baths or showers

Bathing regularly removes dirt from the pores of the skin, which can block them causing spots. It also stops unpleasant smells from developing in places, such as genital areas and armpits. Fresh sweat is mainly water and does not smell much. However, bacteria will cause stale sweat to smell as they thrive in warm, moist conditions. Washing gets rid of the bacteria.

Importance of clean clothing

It does not matter bathing regularly if you put on dirty clothes afterwards. The dirty clothes will have absorbed sweat and will start smelling as bacteria will continue to grow in them.

As well as personal hygiene, there are other factors you need to make choices about in order to lead a healthy lifestyle.

Balanced diet

Eating the right types of food in the right quantities will help you to stay healthy (see page 128).

Exercise

Taking regular exercise, helps you to maintain a healthy weight, and enables you to enjoy an active lifestyle.

Figure 4.10b Taking regular exercise makes you feel healthy and strong

Rest

Getting enough rest is also an essential part of a healthy lifestyle. Many young people do not get enough sleep. They can be distracted by playing electronic games, visiting social networking sites and surfing the internet. This leads to poor attention spans the next day and can make a person more susceptible to diseases.

Key points

- Personal hygiene is important to prevent diseases and for a person to be socially acceptable.

- A healthy life style can lengthen your life span and improve your quality of life.

Summary questions

1 Why is it important to brush your teeth well?

2 Make a list of the important aspects of a healthy lifestyle.

3 a Using your list from question 2, give yourself a mark out of 10 for each aspect of a healthy lifestyle based on your daily activities.

  b Now write down two things you will start (or stop) doing to improve the quality of your lifestyle.

4.11 Food nutrients

Figure 4.11a It is important that we are aware of the impact of diet on our health

Did you know?

About two-thirds of your body is water.

Here are the different types of food nutrients:

Carbohydrates – These are sugars and starch. They provide the energy our cells need. Sweet foods are rich in sugar. We get starch from rice, pasta, bread, yams and cassava.

Proteins – These are needed for growth and repair of cells. We get our protein by eating meat, fish, eggs, milk, nuts and beans.

Fats and oils – These are stores of energy. They also help to keep your body warm. Fats and oils are used to fry foods. They are in margarine, butter, cooking oil and any food made with them, such as cakes, pastries and biscuits.

Vitamins and minerals – Vitamins and minerals help your body perform vital functions (called your metabolism). We only need small amounts of the different vitamins and minerals. Without them, you can get a deficiency disease (see page 122). Fruit and green vegetables have lots of vitamins. For example, oranges give us vitamin C. The mineral calcium, found in milk, is needed for healthy teeth and bones.

Water – Water dissolves the substances that need to move around your body. It also helps to cool your body when you sweat.

Fibre – Fibre helps move solid waste through the alimentary canal and out of your body.

Remember this

The different types of nutrients we get from food are:

- carbohydrates
- proteins
- fats/oils
- vitamins
- minerals
- water
- fibre.

Food tests

Some foods are rich in one type of nutrient. For example, rice, bread and pasta are good sources of the carbohydrate, starch.

We can identify the nutrients in food by doing some simple food tests.

Starch

We test for the carbohydrate starch using iodine solution. The reddish brown solution turns blue-black if starch is in the food.

Activity

What's in your food?

Test a variety of foods for starch, simple sugars, proteins and fats as described opposite.

Write up your investigation as shown in Module 1.

You also used this test to find out whether photosynthesis had occurred (see pages 80–81).

Simple (reducing) sugars

Sugars are also carbohydrates. We can test for simple sugars using Benedict's solution. This is a blue solution. When we use a water bath to heat a solution containing a simple sugar, the Benedict's solution turns orange or red.

Proteins

If a food contains protein it will turn blue Biuret solution violet.

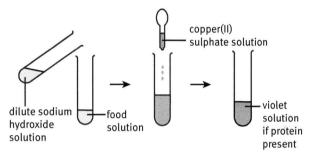

Figure 4.11b Biuret solution turns from blue to violet in a soluble protein

Fats

Put the food on a piece of filter paper and squash it. Scrape the food off. A greasy (translucent) spot will show that the food contains fat.

Key points

- A balanced diet must contain adequate amounts of each food nutrient.

- The nutrients we get from food are: carbohydrates; proteins; fats/oils; vitamins; minerals; water and fibre.

- Food tests: Starch turns iodine solution blue-black; Benedict's solution turns orange/red when heated with a simple sugar; Biuret solution turns violet with protein. Fats leave a greasy mark on filter paper.

School-Based Assessment

You can be assessed on your 'Manipulation and Measurement' and your 'Recording and Communicating' skills in this investigation.

Summary questions

1 Name a good source of:
    a protein b vitamin C c carbohydrate d fat.
2 Why do we need the following nutrients?
    a protein b carbohydrate c fat?
3 Describe how you would carry out the tests for:
    a simple sugars b starch c protein d fat.

4.12 A balanced diet

Figure 4.12a The Caribbean food groups are a guide to a healthy diet

We need to eat a balanced diet to stay healthy. A balanced diet contains adequate amounts of all the essential food nutrients we need.

Look at the poster from the Pan American Health Organisation in Figure 4.12a.

The pie chart shows how we can classify typical Caribbean foods. It also shows the recommended proportions of each needed for a balanced diet.

People who eat an 'unbalanced' diet over a significant time will become malnourished. There are various types of malnutrition:

● the deficiency diseases mentioned in 4.9

● obesity (excess energy intake)

● Protein-energy malnutrition (insufficient protein and energy intake).

Obesity

In the Caribbean (and in many other parts of the world), a growing number of people are becoming obese. Obese people are very overweight, with a body mass index (BMI) over 30. A person's BMI is calculated by dividing their mass in kilograms by their height in metres, squared.

Too much fried food is not good for you and should be avoided. Your body stores fat under your skin and around the organs of your body. Fatty deposits can line the inside of your arteries, increasing the risk of:

– Type 2 diabetes

– heart disease

– high blood pressure.

All of these conditions are very serious. Eating too much saturated animal fat is their main cause.

How much energy do we need?

In order to lose weight, people must use up more energy than the energy that is in the food they eat. But how much energy a person needs each day varies. It depends on:

● your age

● whether you are male or female

● how much physical activity you do.

Malnutrition

Write a newspaper article about the dangers of malnutrition e.g. obesity, anorexia or bulimia.

Person	Energy requirements each day (kJ/day)
Pregnant woman	10 000
Teenage boy	12 500
Man doing manual work	15 000
Young girl	8500
Inactive man over 50 years old	8500
Inactive woman over 50 years old	6750

People require less energy as they get older. Their metabolic rate slows down and they tend to be less active. Young people need more energy to make new proteins for growth. They use up lots of energy when they play.

However, there is concern that young people are doing less physical activity than in the past. This and over-eating mean that childhood obesity is now more common.

Protein-energy malnutrition (PEM)

Starvation causes PEM. Starving children can have a swollen abdomen, with retarded growth and muscle wastage.

Without enough energy being taken in, the body starts to break down protein for energy. This also happens with eating disorders, such as anorexia and bulimia.

Summary questions

1 List the six Caribbean food groups.

2 Which of the Caribbean food groups would be good sources of:

   a protein

   b starch

   c vitamins

   d protein for vegetarians?

3 What are the health problems caused by obesity?

4 Put the following in order of daily energy requirements, starting with most energy:

   a bed-ridden 70 year old; a sprinter in training; a 9 year old girl; a pregnant woman

5 Name two symptoms caused by protein-energy malnutrition.

Key points

- A balanced diet is the daily intake of the right amounts of each nutrient.

- A balanced diet depends on a person's age, activity levels and gender.

- The Caribbean food groups are a guide to a healthy diet.

- Starvation results in PEM.

4.13 Blood

In humans the circulatory system transports substances around the body. The circulatory systems is made up of blood, blood vessels and the heart.

What is blood?

Blood is a mixture made up of:

- plasma
- platelets
- red blood cells
- white blood cells.

Figure 4.13a shows the composition of blood.

The table below describes the function of each part of the blood.

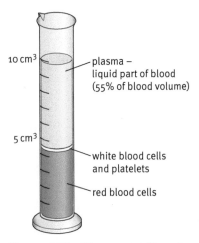

Figure 4.13a The composition of blood

10 cm³ — plasma – liquid part of blood (55% of blood volume)

5 cm³

white blood cells and platelets

red blood cells

Component of blood	Function
Plasma	This straw coloured watery liquid makes up most of the blood. It contains the red blood cells and white blood cells. It also contains small bits of cells called **platelets**. These help in clotting the blood. Plasma transports carbon dioxide, digested food material, waste products, hormones and heat, around your body.
Red blood cells red blood cell cell membrane haemoglobin Figure 4.13b Red blood cells	These 'biconcave discs' carry oxygen from the lungs to cells all round the body. The oxygen bonds temporarily to the red blood cells. The oxygen is released at tissues.
White blood cells lobed nucleus large nucleus phagocyte lymphocyte Figure 4.13c Phagocyte and lymphocyte	These help to protect us against disease. There are two types of white blood cell – phagocytes which engulf pathogens and lymphocytes which produce antibodies to destroy pathogens. These form our immune system.

The blood vessels

There are three types of blood vessel to carry blood around your body:

- arteries – to carry blood away from your heart
- veins – to carry blood back to your heart
- capillaries – to link the arteries and veins

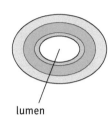

Artery
- thick muscular wall, capable of constricting
- small lumen
- transports blood from the heart (oxygenated except in the pulmonary artery)
- blood under high pressure, moving rapidly, in pulses

lumen (opening)

Vein
- thin muscular wall, with no constriction
- large lumen
- transports blood to the heart (deoxygenated except in the pulmonary vein)
- blood flows slowly, under low pressure

lumen

Capillary
- no muscle
- large lumen
- no constriction
- links arteries to veins
- blood changes from oxygenated to deoxygenated
- flows slowly, under reducing pressure

lumen

Figure 4.13d Structure of the artery, vein and capillary

Key points

- Blood is a liquid tissue that is made up of cells suspended in watery plasma.
- Blood is essential for carrying substances around the body, controlling our body temperature and fighting disease.

Summary questions

1 a What makes up most of your blood?
   b Which part of your blood helps you fight infections?
   c Which part of your blood delivers oxygen to your cells?
   d What is the role of platelets in your blood?

2 Draw a table to summarise the structure and function of the different blood vessels of the body.

4.14 The circulatory system

The human circulatory system is made up of:

- the heart
- the blood
- the various blood vessels (arteries, veins and capillaries).

The heart

The heart is a muscular organ that pumps the blood around your body. It is about the size of your fist. Figure 4.14a shows its structure.

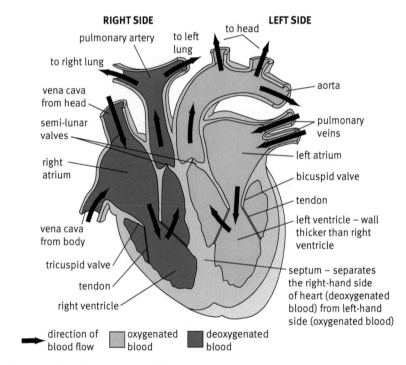

Figure 4.14a The structure of the heart

- The heart acts as a double pump. The right hand side pumps blood out, and the blood returns to the left hand side.
- Blood comes through veins into the top of the heart.
- Oxygenated blood from the lungs arrives into the left atrium.
- De-oxygenated blood returns to the heart through the right atrium.
- The atria contract to force the blood down into the ventricles.
- Then the ventricles contract to pump the blood out of the heart down the arteries.
- The right ventricle sends de-oxygenated blood to the lungs to receive more oxygen and get rid of carbon dioxide.

Activity

Models

Draw or make models of the parts of the circulatory system.

School-Based Assessment

Your teacher can look at your models to assess your skills in 'Recoding and Communicating'.

- The left ventricles send oxygenated blood to tissues all around the body (so this needs stronger muscle than the right ventricle).
- Valves are needed in the heart to make sure blood flows in the right direction and prevent 'backflow'.

Circulation

Figure 4.14b summarises the circulation of blood in a flow chart:

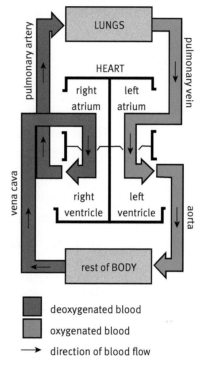

Figure 4.14b Flow chart of the circulatory system

Key points

- The heart pumps blood around the body.
- The heart acts as a double pump.

Summary questions

1 Which artery takes blood to the lungs?

2 Which atrium in the heart receives blood from the lungs?

3 Which ventricle has the thicker muscle? Why?

4 What stops blood back-flowing in the heart?

4.15 Blood groups

Learning outcomes

At the end of this topic you should be able to:

▸ list the different blood groups

▸ explain why care should be taken in blood transfusions

▸ explain what an antigen is.

Antigens are molecules on the surface of cells. They cause an immune response in the body. The response is from **antibodies** in your blood plasma.

Antibodies can attach themselves to the antigens, causing the cells to clump together. The antigens on 'foreign' cells can be recognised as being from outside your body. Your body's antibodies recognise its own antigens so do not bind to them.

Antigens and antibodies in different blood groups

Red blood cells can have different antigens on their surface (cell membrane). There are two types of antigen, labelled as A and B. This means there are four types of blood:

● **A (with just A antigens)**

● **B (with just B antigens)**

● **AB (with both A and B antigens)**

● **O (with no antigens)**

Your blood will make antibodies to attack blood cells of a different blood group from your own. We represent the antibodies by a lower case letter. For example, antigen B will be attacked by antibody b. So if you are blood group B, your blood will have a-type antibodies. It will not have b antibodies or it would attack its own blood.

The table below shows the antigens and antibodies in each blood group:

Blood group	Antigens present on red blood cells	Antibodies present in plasma
A	A	b
B	B	a
AB	A and B	none
O	none	a and b

Blood transfusions

Only certain types of blood can be given to a person after an accident or during an operation. If the wrong type is given, antibodies will attack the red blood cells causing them to clump together. This can lead to death.

Activity

Blood group survey

Carry out a survey of blood groups of people in your class.

Present your results as a bar chart.

The table below shows which blood groups are compatible with each other:

		Blood group of the **recipient (receiver)**			
		A	**B**	**AB**	**O**
Blood group of the donor (giver)	**A**	yes	no	yes	no
	B	no	yes	yes	no
	AB	no	no	yes	no
	O	yes	yes	yes	yes

For example, we can explain the last column in the table. If you are blood group O, you have antibodies of both a and b. So if you are given blood from groups A, B or AB, the red blood cells will stick together and ultimately be broken down. You are incompatible with blood groups A, B and AB. So only a transfusion of blood group O would work.

Blood group AB is the called the **universal recipient**. A person with this blood group can receive any blood group and not be harmed.

Blood group O is called the **universal donor**, because it can be given to persons with any blood group.

Key points

- Blood groups are determined by antigens A and B. Blood group O has no antigens on the red blood cells.

- Blood transfusions can save lives, but the blood groups of the recipient and the donor must be compatible.

- Blood group AB is the universal recipient (people with AB blood can be given any blood group) and O is the universal donor (blood group O can be given to any patient without harming them).

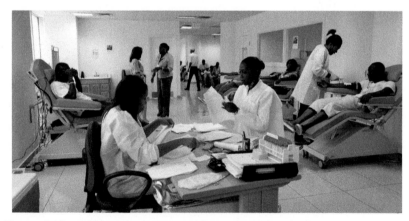

Figure 4.15a A blood donor soon replaces the 500 cm³ of blood donated

Summary questions

1 Name the four blood groups.

2 Which blood group is called the universal donor and which is called the universal recipient? Give reasons for your answer.

3 Explain why someone with blood group A should never receive a blood transfusion from a donor of blood group B.

End of module 4 questions

Your School-Based Assessment for Module 4 will be a 20 question multiple choice test. It will be made up of 4 questions (items) from each of the following topics.

a Reproduction

b Growth and development

c Food

d Drugs

e Diseases

Two of these four questions will measure the Recording and Communicating skills and two will measure the Analysis and Interpretation skills.

Here is a similar test on which you can practise.

1 Following fertilisation, the ball of cells that implants on the wall of the uterus and starts to grow there is called:

  a a baby

  b an embryo

  c a foetus

  d a zygote

2 From which of the following structures is an egg (ovum) released each month?

  a Fallopian tube

  b Uterus

  c Cervix

  d Ovary

Items **3–4** refer to the graph opposite which shows the number of pregnancies occurring in one year for groups of couples using various methods of contraception.

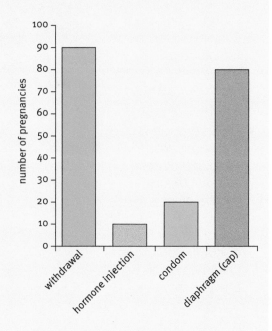

3 Which is the LEAST effective contraceptive methods used by these couples?

  a Condom

  b Withdrawal

  c Diaphragm (cap)

  d Hormone injection

4 Which contraceptive method resulted in approximately 80 per cent of the couples in the group becoming pregnant?

 a Condom

 b Withdrawal

 c Diaphragm

 d Hormone injection

Items **5–7** refer to the table below which shows the results of food tests carried out on five food samples.

Food sample	Violet colour present	Blue black	Greasy (translucent) mark	Red-orange precipitate
A	✓		✓	
B		✓		
C			✓	
D		✓		✓
E	✓			

5 Which of the food samples contain protein?

 a A and E

 b B and C

 c C and E

 d D and E

6 The blue-black colour for sample B means that it contains

 a fat

 b starch

 c protein

 d simple (reducing) sugar

7 Which of the food sample contains the nutrients needed for a quick energy boost?

 a A

 b B

 c C

 d D

8 Which of the following food tests is used for fat?

  a Biuret   b Iodine

  c Benedict's   d Grease spot

9 The drinking of excessive amounts of alcohol can cause

  a malnutrition

  b severe liver damage

  c lung cancer

  d diabetes

10 In which of the following substances is caffeine found?

  a Coffee

  b Tobacco

  c Marijuana

  d Alcoholic drinks

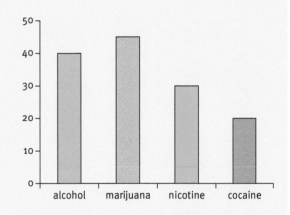

Items **11–12** refer to the graph opposite which shows the numbers of teenagers in a drug rehabilitation programme who experimented with various drugs

11 Which drug was LEAST commonly used by the teenagers in the drug rehabilitation programme?

  a Alcohol

  b Cocaine

  c Nicotine

  d Marijuana

12 The number of teenagers in the drug rehabilitation programme who took marijuana is

  a 30

  b 35

  c 40

  d 45

13 Mrs Brown was complaining of feeling tired all the time. A blood test showed that she had

  a anaemia

  b leukaemia

  c dengue fever

  d haemophilia

Question 14 refers to the chart opposite which shows the percentage of deaths from various diseases in a Caribbean island.

14 Which of the following types of disease is responsible for the least number of the deaths in this island?

   a Inherited

   b Infectious

   c Nutritional

   d Physiological

15 Lack of insulin in the blood may cause

   a cancer

   b scurvy

   c anaemia

   d diabetes

16 Which of the following is NOT a nutritional disease?

   a Anaemia   b Rickets

   c Goitre   d Sickle cell anaemia

17 Which of the following blood groups is that of the 'Universal recipient' (receiver)?

   a A   b B

   c O   d AB

18 Which of the following components of blood transports oxygen around the body?

   a Plasma

   b Platelets

   c Red blood cells

   d White blood cells

19 Which of the following describes an artery?

   a Thin muscular walls

   b Thick muscular walls

   c Large lumen

   d Presence of valves

20 In an extreme emergency where a man needed an immediate blood transfusion, which blood would it be best to give him to save his life?

   a A   b B

   c O   d AB

At the end of this topic you should be able to:

▸ list the forms of energy

▸ explain the concept of energy

▸ identify the forms of energy involved in a given object or situation.

Energy can be thought of as the ability to do work. Nothing would happen without energy. Just think of all the activities you do in a day. Even when you are asleep, your body needs energy to keep you alive.

There are different forms of energy. These are the main forms:

- **Electrical energy** – this is the energy transferred when an electric current flows around a circuit
- **Kinetic energy** – this is the energy an object has due to its movement
- **Potential energy** – this is stored energy – for example, when an object is positioned above the ground (often called gravitational potential energy) or when a rubber band is stretched (often called elastic or strain potential energy)
- **Chemical energy** – the energy stored in substances, such as fuels and food, which is released in chemical reactions
- **Sound energy** – energy transferred by sound waves
- **Light energy** – energy transferred by light waves
- **Nuclear energy** – the energy released from the centre (nucleus) of atoms when radioactivity is produced
- **Solar energy** – energy from the Sun
- **Heat energy** – energy due to the temperature of an object

Activity

Identifying forms of energy

Look at Figures 5.1a to 5.1e and discuss which is the main form of energy involved in each one.

Working in a small group, design a game to help you remember the different forms of energy.

Figure 5.1a A bungee jumper about to jump

Figure 5.1b A cricket fan

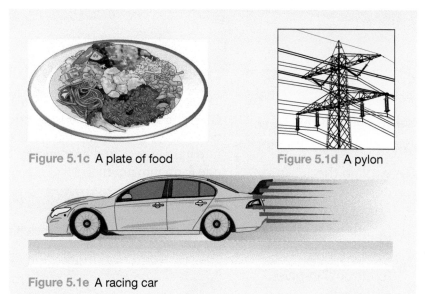

Figure 5.1c A plate of food

Figure 5.1d A pylon

Figure 5.1e A racing car

Remember this

Nothing would happen without energy!

Key points

- The main forms of energy are electrical, kinetic, potential, chemical, sound, light, nuclear, solar and heat energy.
- Energy is the ability to do work.
- All activities require energy in order to take place.

Summary questions

1 Write a definition of energy.

2 Explain three forms of energy involved in getting ready for school.

3 Identify the main form of energy linked to statements a–f below:

   a a speedboat in action

   b an elevator at the top floor of a hotel

   c sunbathers on a beach

   d a football travelling along the ground on its way into the goal

   e the most powerful bombs, first made in the Second World War

   f a box of fireworks.

5.2 Energy conversions

Conservation of energy

Think about what happens when you turn on an electric light bulb. Once the switch is pressed, electrical energy is carried through wires to the bulb. Inside the bulb, this electrical energy is changed into light energy and heat energy. So energy can be changed from one form into another.

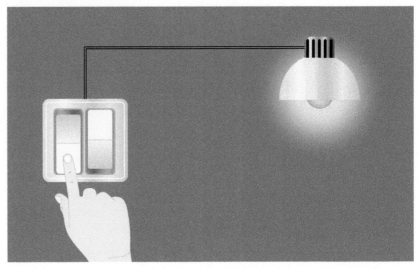

Figure 5.2a Energy can change from one form to another to make things happen

Scientists have looked at lots of energy changes, like lighting a bulb, and have carefully measured the total energy before and after the change. They find that:

the total energy before a change = the total energy after a change

This happens because **energy cannot be created or destroyed**. This is called the conservation of energy.

We can show the energy change (conversion) when a light bulb is switched on like this:

electrical energy $\longrightarrow$ light energy + heat energy

The heat energy is wasted energy. We switch the bulb on to light up the room, not to heat it up. Scientists have found that some energy is wasted in all energy changes.

Other energy changes

a) A fairground ride

Some fairground rides are like giant pendulums. They swing back and forth, suspended on a single pivot. At the top of each swing, the ride stops for a split second before plunging downwards, then up to the other side.

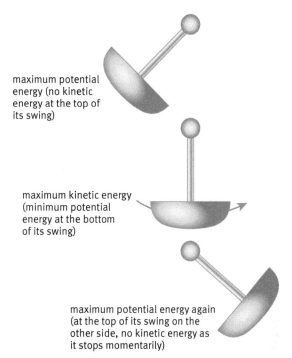

maximum potential energy (no kinetic energy at the top of its swing)

maximum kinetic energy (minimum potential energy at the bottom of its swing)

maximum potential energy again (at the top of its swing on the other side, no kinetic energy as it stops momentarily)

Figure 5.2b Converting between potential and kinetic energy at a fairground

The energy change in the fairground ride is:

potential → kinetic → potential → kinetic
energy   energy   energy   energy... and so on

The ride will eventually stop because some energy is wasted on every swing which is not shown above. Heat energy is also produced because of friction (of the moving parts of the ride at the pivot and of air resistance as the ride moves).

b) Watching television

Figure 5.2c Electrical energy is a convenient way of transferring energy from one place to another where it is changed into other forms of energy

When you watch television, the energy change can be shown as:

electrical → light energy + sound energy + heat energy
energy

Continued

The unwanted, wasted energy is heat energy.

The less energy wasted when we use an electrical appliance, the more efficient the machine is.

Here are some more examples of energy conversions:

c) Shining a torch

The flow diagram below (called an energy transfer diagram) shows the energy changes that take place in a torch:

chemical energy ⟶ **electrical energy** ⟶ **heat + light**
in the batteries　　　 **in the wires**　　　　　 **from the lamp**

Figure 5.2d Batteries are stores of chemical energy, ready to convert it to electrical energy

Batteries and cells store energy in the chemicals inside them. The chemicals are chosen because they can transfer their chemical energy into electrical energy as they react together. The electrical energy is converted to heat energy inside the torch's bulb (wasted energy) and light energy (useful energy).

The chemicals in the battery will eventually run out and the reaction that releases electrical energy will no longer take place. Then the batteries have to be disposed of safely or if re-chargeable will need to be put in their charger and plugged into the mains electricity supply to regenerate the original chemicals again.

d) Going up in an elevator

This is the energy transfer diagram for an elevator:

electrical energy ⟶ **kinetic energy** ⟶ **gravitational**
from the mains　　　 **as motor spins**　　　 **potential energy**
　　　　　　　　　　　　and elevator moves　**as it rises up**

The electrical energy from the mains supply operates a strong electric motor that lifts the heavy elevator attached to strong metal cables. As the elevator rises it gains gravitational potential energy.

Figure 5.2e As soon as the elevator starts its ascent its gravitational potential energy increases with its height

Figure 5.2f There are three nuclear power sites in Florida, USA

e) Using solar panels

solar energy ⟶ **heat energy stored in water**
from the sun   **inside the solar panel system**

Solar panels use energy radiated directly from the sun to heat the water that circulates through the black panels you see on some roofs. You can see solar panels on page 159.

f) A nuclear power station

Here are the energy changes in an nuclear power station that generates electricity:

nuclear energy ⟶ **heat energy** ⟶ **kinetic energy** ⟶ **electrical**
               in steam   **of turbines in**   **energy**
                             generator

There are no nuclear reactors generating electricity in the Caribbean at present, but there a five in the state of Florida, at three different sites. There are issues with nuclear power stations because of the potentially disastrous consequences of accidents at these plants.

School-Based Assessment

Your teacher will assess your skills in Social Attributes (SA) in this activity. You will need to show respect for others in your group and take responsibility for completing your part of the task. Make sure you collaborate on decisions and cooperate with the rest of your group.

Activity

Everyday energy

a Carry out some research to find out how the efficiency of appliances is shown on packaging.

- Draw a poster to illustrate your findings.

b Research the impact of energy conversions on everyday activities, such as transport, entertainment or sport.

- Produce a written report or oral presentation and share your findings in a presentation.

Key points

- Energy is neither created nor destroyed; it only changes from one form to another.

- Some energy is wasted in useful energy conversions, often as heat energy.

Summary questions

1 What do we mean by the term 'conservation of energy'?

2 Show the energy changes when a motor car is moving along a road.

3 A bungee jumper uses elastic (or strain) energy in a stretched rubber rope to bounce up at the bottom of their jump.

  a Show the energy changes involved in a bungee jump.

  b Why does the bungee jumper eventually stop bouncing at the end of the rubber rope?

5.3 Conduction

Learning outcomes

At the end of this topic you should be able to:

▸ describe situations in which energy is transferred by conduction

▸ discuss the importance of heat conduction.

As well as energy being converted from one form to another, energy can be transferred from one place to another.

Heat energy can be transferred by conduction, convection and radiation.

Transferring heat energy by conduction

Whenever food is cooked in a pan, heat energy is transferred by conduction.

In Module 2 we found that metals are good conductors of heat energy. They allow heat energy to pass through them easily.

Pans are usually made of copper, steel or aluminium metals.

Figure 5.3a Pans are made of metal because they are good conductors of heat energy, so heat travels from the source of energy into the food easily

You can test which of these metals, aluminium, steel or copper, is the best conductor of heat energy by carrying out the experiment below.

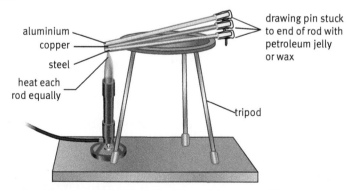

Figure 5.3b The rod with the drawing pin which drops off first will be the best conductor of heat energy

Substances conduct heat by passing on extra vibrations from atom to atom. Metals can also use their free electrons, which are not bound to any one atom, to transfer heat energy. These can move quickly through the metal, carrying the heat energy with them.

Pan handles are made of an insulator, such as wood or hard plastic, so you do not burn your hand when picking up a hot pan. Insulators contain no free electrons, so heat energy does not spread as quickly through an insulator as it does through a metal.

Liquids are *not* good conductors of heat energy as shown by the experiment below.

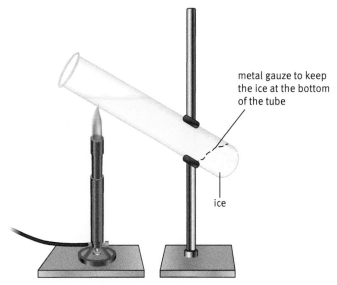

metal gauze to keep the ice at the bottom of the tube

ice

Figure 5.3c The ice cube does not melt quickly despite the heat energy supplied at the top of the water in the tube

Key points

- Conduction is the transfer of heat energy through substances.
- Metals are good conductors of heat energy.
- Conduction is important in everyday life, for example in cooking.

Summary questions

1 Which of these substances are good conductors of heat energy and which are good insulators?

   iron, gold, wood, glass, steel, lead, plastic

   Show your answer in a table.

2 Explain why certain materials are chosen to make a pan.

3 Explain why metals are good conductors of heat energy.

5.4 Convection

Learning outcomes

At the end of this topic you should be able to:

▸ to describe situations in which energy is transferred by convection

▸ discuss the importance of heat convection.

The second way that heat energy can be transferred is by convection.

Convection is the transfer of heat energy by the movement of fluids.

A fluid is a liquid or a gas. Whenever we heat a fluid, heat energy moves around the fluid by convection currents. You might have seen birds gliding in the sky. They use convection currents in the air to give them lift.

Figure 5.4a Birds can glide on convection currents in the air (called thermals)

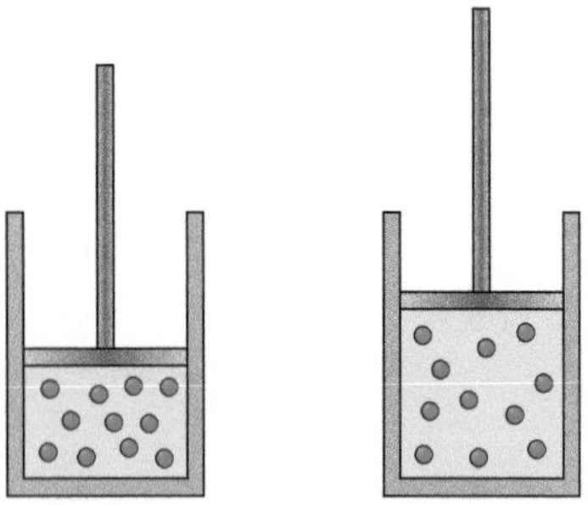

When a fluid is heated its particles move around more quickly. This means that a given number of particles will take up more space.

Remember this

When a fluid is heated it expands because of the increased movement of its particles – the particles themselves DO NOT expand.

Gas at 20°C   Same gas at 40°C

Figure 5.4b A hot fluid takes up a larger volume than when it is cold – so the hot fluid has a lower density

As the fluid warms up, it expands and its density decreases. This means that the hot part of the fluid will rise. It floats upwards. The heat energy is transferred by the hot particles moving from a warmer place to a cooler place. We call this convection.

As the warmer particles rise, cooler ones move sideways to take their place. This in turn makes particles in the fluid move downwards to take their place and a cycle is set up. This is how convection currents form in fluids.

A convection current can be seen in a large beaker of water heated by a Bunsen burner. Adding a coloured crystal allows us to see the movement of the water.

Look at the diagram of the experiment at the top of the next page. The large beaker is heated gently on a tripod and gauze.

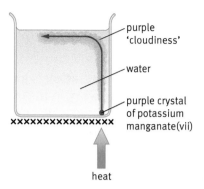

Figure 5.4c A convection current can be set up in a beaker of water

Land and sea breezes

The wind near the coast often blows in from the sea in the daytime (a sea breeze). Look at Figure 5.4d. Then, at night, it blows out to sea (a land breeze). These land and sea breezes are caused by convection currents in the air.

Figure 5.4d Convection currents causing a sea breeze

In sunlight, the land warms up more quickly than the sea. So the air above the land rises. Cooler air from over the sea rushes inland to take its place. So in daytime we get a breeze coming in off the sea.

At night-time, the land cools down more quickly than the sea. So the warmer air above the sea rises. Then the cooler air from over the land rushes out to take its place. This produced a breeze out to sea from the land.

Remember this

It is a hot gas or liquid that rises in convection – so do not say that 'heat' rises.

Key points

- Convection is the transfer of heat energy by the movement of fluid (liquid or gas).

- A hotter fluid rises, and a cooler fluid moves in to take its place.

- Convection currents can cause winds near the coast.

Summary questions

1 How is heat energy transferred through a fluid by convection?

2 Explain how a night-time land breeze arises at the coast. Include a diagram in your answer.

3 Explain how a convection current is set up in a room heated by a radiator against one wall. Include a diagram in your answer.

5.5 Radiation

Radiation is another way of transferring heat energy. It transfers energy in the form of invisible waves, such as infrared radiation. These waves are given off from any hot object. You can feel radiated heat energy when you hold your hands near a fire.

You might have seen images taken at night using an infrared camera. These cameras detect infrared radiation given off from objects. The hotter the object, the more infrared radiation it gives off (emits).

Figure 5.5a The police and army use 'night-vision' cameras to detect people in the dark

Radiation does not need a substance to transfer heat energy, unlike conduction and convection. That is why it can travel through space which is a vacuum (contains no particles). The Sun's energy travels through space to reach Earth by radiation.

In experiments with shiny, silvery cans and dull, black cans of water, scientists find that:

a) a dull, black can of cold water warms up faster than a shiny, silvery can containing the same volume of water in sunlight, and

b) a dull, black can of hot water cools down faster than a shiny, silvery one.

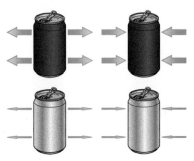

Figure 5.5b The differences in giving off and absorbing radiation between dull black and shiny silver surfaces

This shows that:

- **dull, black surfaces absorb radiation more quickly than a shiny, silvery surface**
- **dull, black surfaces radiate heat energy more quickly than a shiny, silvery surface.**

You have now seen conduction, convection and radiation in action. The next activity compares their effectiveness in cooking potatoes.

Activity

Cooking potatoes

Compare the different methods of transferring heat energy as ways of cooking potatoes.

- Conduction – shallow frying with a little oil in a frying pan
- Convection – boiling in a pan of water
- Radiation – Roasting in an oven or grill (or in a microwave oven)

Write up this investigation as shown in Module 1. Make sure you use your knowledge about conduction, convection and radiation to explain your results.

School-Based Assessment

Your teacher will be looking at your skills of Analysis and Interpretation (AI) in this investigation.

Remember this

Radiation does not need another substance (or medium) to pass through to transfer energy. It can travel through a vacuum.

Key points

- Radiation is the energy released from hot objects.
- Radiation can transfer heat energy through a vacuum, for example when heat energy travels from the Sun to Earth.

Summary questions

1 Why is it fortunate for life on Earth that radiation can travel through a vacuum?

2 Classify the following examples of heat transfer as conduction, convection or radiation:

 a toasting a piece of bread

 b a hot water system in a house

 c burgers frying on a hot-plate

 d a sea breeze at the coast.

5.6 Energy sources

Non-renewable energy sources

Fossil fuels

Coal, oil and natural gas are called fossil fuels. They are found beneath the ground or the seabed. Fossil fuels are non-renewable sources of energy. They have taken millions of years to form.

As these fossil fuels start to run out, the following alternative forms of renewable energy will become increasingly important. Renewable energy sources will not run out.

Renewable energy sources

Solar energy

This is energy from the Sun. It can be used in solar cells which transform the Sun's energy to electrical energy. Alternatively, it can be used directly to heat water for use at home using solar panels.

Biofuels

Biofuels come from plants or animals. We can either use the plant or animal material directly, as with wood, or use their products, as with biogas. Bagasse is the pulpy remains left after the juice is removed from sugar cane stalks. It is a useful fuel.

Wood-chip can be used to heat homes or generate electricity. New trees are planted to replace the ones cut down to burn as fuels.

Biogas is made from the waste products of farm animals and humans, as well as waste vegetation. The waste is collected into special biogas generators where microorganisms break down the waste materials to form the biogas.

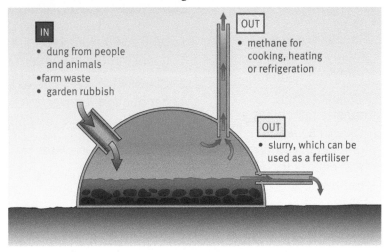

Figure 5.6a A biogas generator is best installed beneath the ground where they are well insulated, as they work best at about 30°C

Figure 5.6b Wind turbines are useful in windy places

Crops are also specially grown to make fuel for vehicles. This biodiesel is made from vegetable oils extracted from crops such as maize, oilseed rape, and palm.

Ethanol is another liquid biofuel. It is produced by the fermentation of sugar from crops, such as sugar cane, using yeast. It can be mixed with petrol and sold as 'gasohol' to run cars.

Wind energy

On high ground, near the coast, or even out at the sea, wind turbines are becoming more common. The huge blades of the wind turbines are positioned facing the wind. They catch the wind and spin or rotate round. This provides the energy to generate electricity.

Wave energy

The movement of waves across the sea, caused by the wind, can be used to make electricity. Floats can rock up and down to harness the energy of the waves.

Geothermal energy

This uses energy from hot rocks beneath the Earth's surface. Water is piped down to areas where the hot rocks are not too deep and steam returns to the surface. The steam is used to drive turbines to generate electricity, as in conventional fossil fuel power stations.

Hydroelectric energy

Hydroelectric energy uses the gravitational, potential energy stored in water held in a dam. The water is allowed to fall to a lower level and on the way down turns the turbines to generate electricity

Key points

- Non-renewable energy resources cannot be replaced in a reasonable time; so with continued use, they will run out.
- Renewable energy sources will not run out/be used up.
- Renewable energy sources include solar energy and geothermal energy.

Summary questions

1 What do we mean by 'non-renewable' and 'renewable' energy sources?

2 Describe how the following produce energy for us to use:

  a wind energy   b hydroelectric energy

  c wave energy   d geothermal energy.

5.7 More about fossil fuels

Learning outcomes

At the end of this topic you should be able to:

▸ define the term fossil fuel

▸ discuss the effects of fossil fuels on the environment.

Formation of fossil fuels

Most of our common fuels are fossil fuels:

- coal
- crude oil (which gives us petrol and diesel)
- natural gas.

Fossil fuels have taken millions of years to form. Coal came from trees and ferns that died and were buried beneath swamps about 300 million years ago.

Crude oil was formed from tiny sea animals and plants which lived about 150 million years ago. They were buried under layers of sand and silt on the sea bed. They did not decay normally as there was hardly any oxygen there. The increased pressure and temperature changed them into oil. Natural gas is usually found with crude oil.

The plants and animals that formed fossil fuels originally got their energy from the Sun. This became stored as chemical energy in the fossil fuel. So when you burn a fuel you are using energy that started off in the Sun.

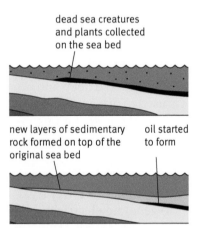

dead sea creatures and plants collected on the sea bed

new layers of sedimentary rock formed on top of the original sea bed

oil started to form

Figure 5.7a The formation of crude oil and natural gas

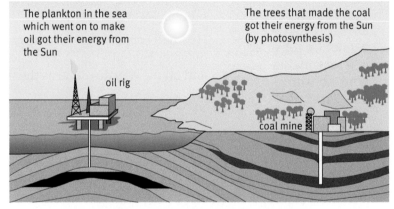

The plankton in the sea which went on to make oil got their energy from the Sun

The trees that made the coal got their energy from the Sun (by photosynthesis)

oil rig

coal mine

Figure 5.7b The energy stored in fossil fuels originated from the Sun

Problems caused by fossil fuels

Most fossil fuels contain sulphur impurities. When we burn the fuel, the sulphur turns into sulphur dioxide (SO_2) gas. Power stations burning coal or oil give off most sulphur dioxide. This is the main cause of acid rain.

Cars burning petrol or diesel also contribute to making our rain acidic.

The effects of acid rain

- Forests – trees are damaged and even killed.
- Fish – hundreds of lakes now have no fish left in them at all.

Aluminium in the soil gets washed into the lakes by acid rain. This poisons the fish.

- Buildings – acid rain attacks buildings and metal structures. Limestone buildings are most badly affected.

Global warming

The Earth's atmosphere acts like a greenhouse. As you learnt in topic 3.14, gases, such as carbon dioxide, absorb some heat energy given off as the Earth cools down. This heat energy gets trapped in the atmosphere and cannot escape out into space.

However, we are making more and more of these gases. Whenever we burn a fossil fuel we make carbon dioxide.

The extra carbon dioxide seems to be making the Earth hotter. We call this **global warming**. There is great concern in the Caribbean over the effects of global warming. People are worried by the predictions of:

- more hurricanes which are more severe.
- more droughts
- rising sea levels and flooding.

Figure 5.7c Global warming could cause more frequent hurricanes, like Hurricane Deane in 2007

Key points

- Fossil fuels are coal, crude oil and natural gas.
- They are usually found deep underground.
- Burning fossil fuels causes air pollution, which results in problems such as acid rain and global warming.

Summary questions

1 Describe how crude oil was formed.

2 Where does the energy stored in a fossil fuel come from originally?

3 Which gas formed from burning coal in a coal-fired power station can contribute to:

   a acid rain

   b global warming.

4 Find out how long the world's supplies of each type of fossil fuel are expected to last.

5.8 Energy conservation

Learning outcomes

At the end of this topic you should be able to:

▸ list some ways in which we can conserve energy

▸ discuss the need to conserve energy.

We all need to conserve energy. Most of our electricity is produced in power stations that burn fossil fuels. Fossil fuel supplies are limited and will run out eventually, so we should all try to use less. For example, crude oil and natural gas will probably run out in your lifetime. Coal will last longer. Using less fossil fuels will also reduce air pollution.

Electricity is a major household bill. Therefore if people can think of ways to conserve energy it could reduce their electricity bills.

Here are some ways of using less electricity (electrical energy) and saving money:

● switch off lights when they are not in use

● choose energy efficient devices when buying new appliances

● use energy-saving light bulbs in place of traditional filament bulbs (which waste a lot of energy as heat)

Figure 5.8a This type of light bulb saves energy compared with filament light bulbs which waste more energy as heat

● do not leave chargers on when nothing is attached to them

● do not leave televisions on stand-by; turn them off

● select low energy programs when running electrical appliances such as washing machines or dish-washers

● use traditional tools if possible instead of electrical devices when doing work on gardens and homes (and the exercise is good for you)

● shower instead of having a bath as it uses less hot water which is sometimes heated electrically

● do not over-boil food when cooking

● use electrical heating and air conditioning for less time.

We can also use less fuel by using cars less. For example:

- walk or cycle shorter journeys
- take public transport, such as the bus, as this is a more efficient way of using fuel.

Figure 5.8b Cycling instead of riding in a car will save energy and is good exercise!

Activity

Incentives to save energy

A government wants to offer money to those who can invest in energy-saving measures for their homes. Imagine you are a householder and want to claim a grant.

Working in a group, put together a plan for your home that will help you to reduce the energy you use. Think about ways to keep your home warm in cooler weather and cool in warm weather.

Key points

- Conserving energy will reduce household bills.
- Conserving energy means that fossil fuels will last longer.
- Pollution will be reduced by conserving energy.

Summary questions

1 Suggest three things outside the home that you can do to save energy.

2 Why is reducing your electricity bills a good idea for you and the environment?

3 Think of five ways in which your school could conserve more energy.

5.9 Comparing energy sources

Every source of energy has its advantages and disadvantages to consider.

Biofuels

Ethanol, made from sugar cane, could be an excellent fuel to replace petrol. Like biodiesel, it helps reduce carbon dioxide emissions overall, as the plants it is made from absorb carbon dioxide as they grow – even though they still give off carbon dioxide when they burn.

Figure 5.9a Sugar cane can be used as a bio-crop to make ethanol for use as a fuel. It also produces bagasse as a waste product which can also be used as a fuel, for example to help run a sugar mill

Using crops to make fuels means there is less land for food crops. This could raise the cost of basic foods. Also, new land for growing biofuel crops is created by cutting down forests. This will destroy habitats for wildlife.

Wave power

Each float on the surface of the sea can only generate a small amount of energy. Therefore, several miles of floats linked together are needed to generate the same power as a traditional fossil fuel power station.

Tidal power

In some places there are large differences between high and low tides, such as in river estuaries. The movement of the water in and out can turn turbines to generate electricity. A large barrage has to be built across the estuary.

Hydroelectric power

Hydroelectric plants are often in beautiful mountainous areas, so the landscape is spoiled. Large areas of land are often flooded to create the dams needed to store large reservoirs of water. This also destroys wildlife habitats, as well as villages in some cases.

Wind power

The wind turbines only work when there is sufficient wind. The tall towers are unsightly and spoil the natural landscape. The turbines can also be noisy.

Solar power

The Caribbean lies near the equator and has plenty of hours of sunshine per year. Therefore, solar energy is an attractive alternative source of energy.

However, at present it is the most expensive method of generating electricity of the alternative energy options. It has high set up costs and is only 17% efficient, although the energy can be stored. Researchers continue to look for more efficient ways to store the energy and to make solar cells more effective.

Solar panels can use the Sun's energy to heat water in pipes directly.

Figure 5.9b Solar panels will save on electricity bills, but can be expensive to install

Activity

Pros and cons

Working in a pair, choose one energy source and do some further research into its advantages and disadvantages.

- Make a list of your findings to discuss with another pair researching a different energy source.

- Try to decide together which would be the better alternative in the Caribbean.

Key points

- All energy sources have some advantages and some disadvantages.

- Fossil fuels cause pollution and are running out.

- Alternative energy sources can be expensive to set up and might be unreliable.

Summary questions

1 Name two energy sources that are unreliable.

2 Give two disadvantages of using biofuels obtained from plants.

3 Give three alternative energy sources that could be used at a sunny seaside town at the mouth of tidal estuary with strong prevailing winds.

5.10 Electrical conductors and insulators

Learning outcomes

At the end of this topic you should be able to:

▸ explain what a circuit is

▸ define the terms conductor and insulator

▸ classify materials as conductors or insulators

▸ list some uses of conductors and insulators.

Electrical circuits

Electricity can only flow if there is a complete pathway for it to pass around. The unbroken pathway from, and back to, an electrical power supply is called a circuit. The power supply can be a cell, battery, power pack or electrical socket.

The electricity itself is made up of moving electrons (the tiny negative particles from inside atoms – see page 43). Look at the simple electrical circuit in Figure 5.10a. It shows the electrons moving through a circuit made up of a cell and a lamp.

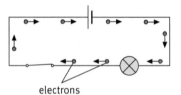

electrons

Figure 5.10a Electrons moving around an electrical circuit

Electrical symbols

We use circuit diagrams to represent circuits. The components in the circuit are each given a symbol. Figure 5.10b shows some common electrical symbols.

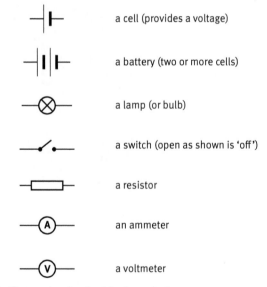

a cell (provides a voltage)

a battery (two or more cells)

a lamp (or bulb)

a switch (open as shown is 'off')

a resistor

an ammeter

a voltmeter

Figure 5.10b Some simple electrical symbols

Conductors and insulators

Conductors allow electricity to pass through them.

Insulators do not allow electricity to pass through them.

The circuit to test which materials are conductors and which are insulators is shown in Figure 5.10c.

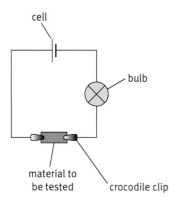

Figure 5.10c The material being tested is put across the gap in the circuit to see if the lamp lights up

- Materials that let electrons flow through them are electrical conductors.
- Materials that do not let electrons pass through them are electrical insulators.

Activity

Testing electrical conductivity

Set up a circuit as in Figure 15.10c and test a variety of items to see which ones are conductors and which are insulators.

Record your results in a table.

We find that all metals are good conductors of electricity, whereas most non-metallic materials are insulators.

Carbon in the form of graphite is an exception as it is a non-metal that does contain electrons that are free to move through its structure.

There are some materials, such as silicon, which will conduct electricity slightly (not as well as a metal but better than an insulator). These are called semi-conductors. They are used to make components used in computers.

Uses of electrical conductors

- Wires in electrical circuits
- Electrical appliances
- Lighting
- Heating and cooking

Uses of electrical insulators

- To protect against electrocution, for example, plastic coating on wires
- Casing for electrical plugs and sockets

Remember this

All metals are good conductors of electricity.

Key points

- Electrical conductors allow an electric current to pass through them, whereas insulators do not.
- All metals are good conductors of electricity.

Summary questions

1 What do you understand by the term 'a complete circuit'?

2 Give two uses of electrical conductors.

3 Give two uses of electrical insulators.

4 Draw a circuit diagram showing a cell, a switch and a lamp and explain how the lamp lights up.

5.11 Electrical safety

DANGER OF DEATH
KEEP OUT

Figure 5.11a Electricity can kill

Electricity is essential for modern-day living. We all use it every day. However, we should remember how dangerous mains electricity can be. An electric shock can kill so from an early age we should be aware of the hazards and how to behave safely.

It is very important that you never touch a bare wire that is plugged into the mains circuit. Here are some other safety rules:

- ensure that your hands are free of moisture when switching electrical appliances on or off
- make sure the mains switch to the house is off when working on domestic wiring
- always get a qualified electrician to carry out electrical repairs
- electricians should wear rubber soled boots and protective clothing
- never overload a socket by attaching too many electrical appliances at once using adapter plugs – this can cause a fire
- use child safety outlet caps in electrical sockets.

Electrical safety devices

Electrical appliances are very useful, but if too much current flows into them they can overheat and cause fires. This is why we use fuses. A fuse contains a thin wire that melts and snaps if too much current passes through it.

Figure 5.11b Fuses have different ratings depending on the power needed to work the appliance. This type of fuse is used inside plugs

The correct fuse rating, for example 3 amp, 5 amp or 13 amp, depends on the power of the appliance and the mains voltage.

A fuse is chosen that will allow this current to pass through, but will 'blow' (melt and snap) if more that the required amount of current surges into the appliance.

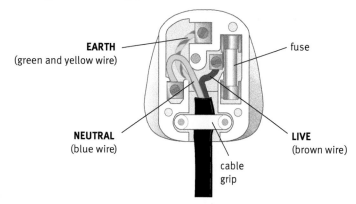

EARTH
(green and yellow wire)

fuse

NEUTRAL
(blue wire)

LIVE
(brown wire)

cable grip

Figure 5.11c The fuse inside a 3-pin plug

Other electrical safety devices include:

- circuit breakers
- surge protectors
- Uninterruptible Power Supply (UPS)
- line conditioners.

Key points

- Electricity is dangerous – an electric shock can kill you.
- Care is needed when using electrical devices powered by mains electricity.
- Electrical safety devices include fuses and circuit breakers.

Summary questions

1 Why should household sockets have plastic protectors inserted when not in use, if there are young children in the home?

2 Describe how a fuse works.

3 What are the different-sized fuses you can get to use inside plugs on electrical appliances?

5.12 Series and parallel circuits

We explained what an electric current is in 5.10. But there are different types of circuit possible. Electrical components, such as lamps, can be arranged in series or parallel circuits.

Series circuits

In a series circuit the components are connected in line with each other. Look at Figure 5.12a:

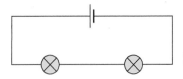

Figure 5.12a Two lamps in series

The current flows through one lamp then the next. We can measure the current using an ammeter. An ammeter connected into a series circuit in any position gives the same reading. This shows that the current is the same at any point in a series circuit.

If one of the lamps in this series circuit is unscrewed or blows, the other lamp goes out too. There is no pathway for the current to make its way back to the other end of the cell. Compare this with the parallel circuit shown in Figure 5.12b:

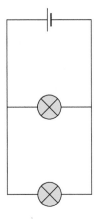

Figure 5.12b Two lamps in parallel

Parallel circuits

In the parallel circuit if one lamp blows, the other stays lit. This is because there is still a complete circuit without the current having to go through the broken branch in the circuit.

The current leaving the cell or battery is split between the branches of the parallel circuit before rejoining again on the way back to the cell.

So if you have a chain of lights it is always best to arrange them in a parallel circuit rather than a series circuit. Then, when one light blows, the rest stay lit. In a series circuit, when one lamp blows, all the lamps go out.

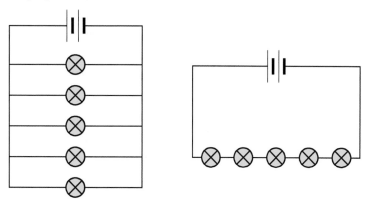

Figure 5.12c It is better to use lamps in parallel (shown on the left) as they work independently

Activity

Making circuits

Using equipment and the circuit diagrams provided by your teacher, make a series circuit and a parallel circuit.

Explore the circuits and write up the investigation in the usual scientific format.

Remember this

In a series circuit you can follow the path of the electric current in its circuit diagram, using your finger, from one end of the power supply to its other end, passing through all the components.
However, in a parallel circuit you will come to junctions where you can go one way or another way.

School-Based Assessment

Your teacher will assess your skills in Analysis and interpretation, as well as Manipulation in this activity.

Key points

- A series circuit has just one path for the electric current to flow around.
- A parallel circuit has alternative routes for the current to flow.

Summary questions

1 Draw a circuit with three bulbs in series.
2 Draw a circuit with three bulbs in parallel.
3 What is the problem with buying a string of lights which are arranged in series?
4 Are the lights at home arranged in series or parallel? Explain how you decided.

5.13 Electricity meters

Most people rely on electrical appliances. However, they have to pay for the electrical energy they use. Electricity boards measure energy consumption using electricity meters in homes. They use a unit of energy called a kilowatt-hour (kWh).

1 kWh is the energy supplied to a 1 kW (1000 W) appliance for 1 hour.

Electricity meters can show either:

● an analogue display (where dials rotate for each digit – see Figure 5.13a)

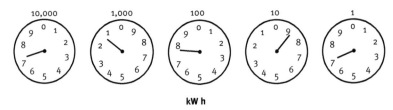

kW h

Figure 5.13a The analogue style meters are being replaced by more modern digital meters. This meter is reading 71787 units of electricity(kWh)

● a digital display (where numbers change and can be read directly – see Figure 5.13b).

Figure 5.13b A digital electricity meter

The electricity supplier will read your meter, perhaps every month, or you can read it and send it in. They will charge you for the number of kilowatt-hours used.

In the worked example at the top of the next page, the charge is divided into two rates called Block 1 and Block 2. A fuel surcharge is also applied to the energy consumed for the first 100 units. Some companies also make a standing charge which must be paid even if you use no electricity.

Worked example

A consumer used 100 units (kWh) of electricity in a month.
The first 50 units were charged on a Block 1 tariff of 60 cents per kWh, and the next 50 units where Block 2 at 70 cents per kWh. The fuel surcharge was 40 cents per kWh used.

What did the consumer pay for their electricity?

Block 1 charge = 60 × 50	= 3000 cents	=	$30.00
Block 2 charge = 70 × 50	= 3500 cents	=	$35.00
Fuel surcharge = 40 × 100 = 4000 cents		= +	$40.00
Total	=		**$105.00**

Activity

Reading your electricity

Read and record your electricity meter at home each day at the same time for two weeks.

- Write up your investigation and show your results on a graph.
- Interpret your results.

School-Based Assessment

Your teacher will assess your skills in Analysis and interpretation in this activity.

Key points

- The amount of electricity used at home is recorded on an electricity meter.
- Analogue meters have dials whereas digital meters show their readings as numbers on LCDs (liquid crystal displays).
- The kilowatt-hour (kWh) is the unit of energy shown on electricity bills and the unit shown on electricity meters.

Summary questions

1 What is the difference between an analogue and a digital electricity meter? Illustrate your answers with examples.

2 A consumer used 200 units (kWh) of electricity in a month.

  50 units were charged on a Block 1 tariff of 60 cents per kWh, and the next 150 were Block 2, charged at 70 cents per kWh.

  The fuel surcharge was 40 cents per kWh used.

  What was the total electricity bill?

5.14 Energy interactions – forces

A force can cause a change in an object. The force may change an object's:

● speed
● direction in which it is moving
● shape.

However, there are still forces acting on objects that are not moving or changing shape.

Activity

Exploring forces

Try some of the activities below and explain them in terms of forces and their effects.

a Marbles hitting each other.

b Dropping objects made of different materials.

c Opening and closing doors.

d Using ramps with different surfaces and angles with toy cars.

e Opening a ring-pull can.

f Twisting modelling clay and a sponge.

Whenever you push an object, the object will push back on you with the same size force, but in the opposite direction.

If a book is placed on a table, a force acts vertically downwards from the book. This is the book's weight, measured in the units of force, **newtons** (N). At the same time, the table pushes vertically upwards on the book with an equal force. We must apply another force to move the book to another position on the table.

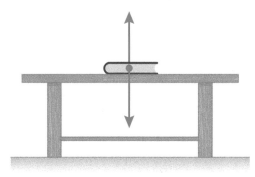

Figure 5.14a We say that the forces on the book are balanced – so it remains stationary on the table

We can represent forces by arrows that point in the direction the force is acting. The length of the arrow is drawn to scale to represent the size of the force. The forces acting at a point can be added up to give a resultant force. If the forces cancel out to give a resultant force of zero, the object is either stationary or moving at a constant velocity.

A jet plane moves forward because its engines push hot gases backwards and the reaction force, called thrust, pushes the plane forward. The thrust is opposed by friction of the plane with the air it moves through (called **air resistance**). The weight of the plane, caused by gravity pulling it downwards, is overcome by lift from air under the wings.

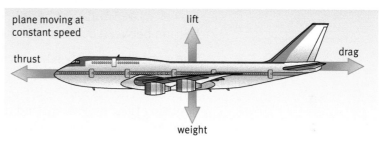

Figure 5.14b The forces acting on a jet plane moving at constant speed at the same height

Key points

- Forces make things move, change direction, speed up, slow down or change shape.

Summary questions

1 Two people on roller blades pull on either end of a rope. Explain what happens.

2 What forces does a plate on a table experience? Why does the plate remain stationary on the desk even though it is experiencing forces?

3 Draw a diagram to show the forces acting on an aeroplane as it travels in a straight line horizontally at a constant speed.

5.15 Types of forces

Learning outcomes

At the end of this topic you should be able to:

▸ state the types of contact forces

▸ state the types of non-contact forces.

Forces can be classified as contact or non-contact forces.

Contact forces

Objects can exert forces on each other by coming into direct contact with each other. For example, these contact forces are involved when we pull, push or twist objects. Contact forces are also involved whenever there is friction.

Friction is bad in some ways, but good in others. Machines waste energy because of the heat energy released through friction. However, we would not be able to walk without the force of friction between our feet and the ground.

The same forces apply when a car moves along a road. If oil is spilt on a road a tyre can no longer grip the road's surface and the force of friction is reduced. The drive wheels spin with no friction opposing their movement and the car skids. The same thing can happen on a wet road or when the tread of tyre is worn down.

Figure 5.15a Wet road surfaces have less friction with tyres than a dry surface

Non-contact forces

Some forces act on objects without the need for objects or materials to be in contact with each other. These include gravity, magnetic and electrostatic forces.

Gravity

Any two objects tend to attract each other. The larger the mass of an object, the stronger its attraction for other objects.

The objects we use in everyday life are too small to notice this attraction. But when you consider an object the size of a planet, then these forces become significant. It is the force of attraction between the objects on Earth and the Earth itself that keeps everything on the surface of the planet. We call this the force of gravity. This force always acts towards the centre of the Earth.

The force of gravity acting on us is called our **weight**, measured in newtons (N), where a mass of 1 kg has a weight of about 10N.

Magnetic force

The area around a bar magnet where magnetic materials feel the force of a magnet is called a magnetic field. Iron filings sprinkled in a magnetic field show there are lines of magnetic force. These are shown to run from the North pole of the magnet to its South pole (see Figure 5.15b).

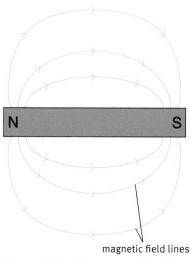

magnetic field lines

Figure 5.15b The magnetic field around a bar magnet

Activity

Bar magnets

a Test a variety of objects with a bar magnet to find out which are attracted.

b Get two bar magnets and experiment with them. Describe how they interact with each other.

Electrostatic force

Positive (+) or negative (–) charges can build up on the surface of some objects. We find that opposite charges attract each other, and like charges repel. So an object carrying a positive charge will attract an object with a negative charge.

Activity

Electrostatic attraction

a Rub an inflated balloon on your jumper and place it near a wall. Describe what happens.

b Rub a plastic ruler on a piece of cloth. Then hold it near a thin jet of water and describe what you observe.

Key points

- There are contact forces and there are non-contact forces.
- Examples of contact forces are twisting, pulling, pushing and friction.
- Examples of non-contact forces are gravity, magnetic and electrostatic forces.

Summary questions

1 List two contact forces and two non-contact forces.

2 What do we mean by the force of:

a friction

b gravity.

3 Draw a diagram to show the magnetic field lines around a bar magnet.

171

End of module 5 questions

1 Look at the diagram of the experiment in the figure opposite.

Predict what you would see in the beaker as it is heated beneath the coloured crystal.

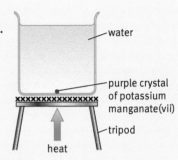

2 a How can we use solar energy to generate electricity in a power station?

 b What would be an ideal place for a solar power station?

 c Why is solar energy not more widely used at present?

3 A match turns chemical energy to heat energy and light energy.

Complete the following energy changes:

 a A falling stone changes _____ energy to _____ energy.

 b A torch changes electrical energy to _____ energy and _____ energy.

 c A car engine changes _____ energy to _____ energy, _____ energy and _____ energy.

 d A mains radio turns _____ energy into _____ energy and _____ energy.

4 Look at the experiment shown opposite:

 a What property is this experiment testing?

 b Describe how the experiment works.

 c The drawing pin fell from rod A in 25 seconds, from rod B in 40 seconds and from rod C in 37 seconds.

   Put these results in a table.

 d What can you conclude from the results of the experiment?

5 Describe, with the aid of a diagram, how a sea breeze arises at the coast.

6 This is a vacuum flask.

 a Does a vacuum flask:

   A Just keep hot drinks hot

   B Just keep cold drinks cold

   C Keeps hot drinks hot, and cold drink cold.

 b Explain how a vacuum flask works.

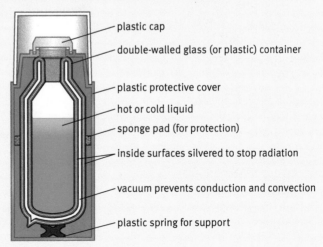

7 This is a biogas generator.

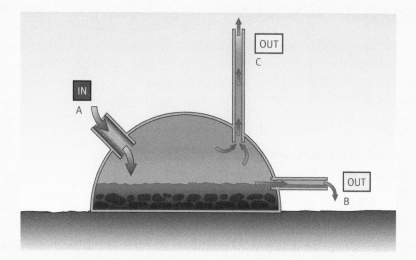

What are the missing labels A, B, and C?

8 a Name three fossil fuels.

b What problems do fossil fuel power stations cause to the environment?

c Why are fossil fuels called non-renewable sources of energy?

9 Identify the energy sources described below:

a uses heat energy from hot rocks beneath the ground

b uses energy from the Sun

c uses energy from water stored in a dam

d uses energy from tiny plants and animals that lived in the sea millions of years ago.

10 Look at the two circuit diagrams below:

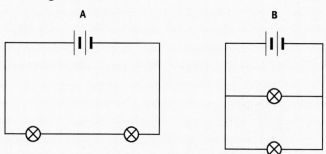

a Which circuit is wired in series and which is in parallel?

b A student unscrews one of the bulbs in each circuit. Describe what happens.

Examination-style practice questions

Module 1 Working like a scientist

1 Which one of the following statements is true?

   a Science and technology are the same.

   b Technology is the application of science.

   c Science is the study of living things and the world around them.

   d Technologists' main aim is to discover new facts about the natural world.

2 A toxic substance is used in a box of pesticide. Which of the following hazard symbols would be displayed on the box?

   a

   b

   c

   d

3 What should you always do after carrying out an experiment with chemicals in a laboratory?

   a Tie your hair back

   b Put on a lab coat

   c Wash your hands

   d Put on safety spectacles

4 Which of the following should be included in your discussion at the end of a scientific investigation?

   a Prediction and hypothesis

   b Results and method/plan

   c Conclusion and evaluation

   d Aim and apparatus

5 Which of the following is a hypothesis?

   a Hot air will rise above cold air because hot air is less dense.

   b Always leave a Bunsen burner with a yellow flame when it is not in use.

   c Measure 5 cm^3 of solution in a measuring cylinder.

   d To find which plastic bag is the strongest.

6 Two students did an investigation to find out how the height from which a ball is dropped affects how high it bounces.

In their investigation, what was the independent variable?

a The height the ball bounces

b The mass of the ball

c The height from which the ball is dropped

d The surface onto which the ball is dropped

7 In an investigation to find out which type of sugar dissolved fastest in water, information about the dependent variable is found by measuring the:

a temperature of the water

b time it takes the sugar to dissolve

c mass of the sugar used

d volume of water used.

8 What would be best way to display the results from the sugar investigation in question 7?

a A table and a bar chart   b A table and a line graph

c A table and a pie chart   d A table only

9 What would you use to measure the temperature of a beaker of boiling water?

a A Bunsen burner   b An electric balance

c A measuring cylinder   d A thermometer

10 A group of students investigated how the temperature of water affected the time it takes for salt to dissolve in water.

They found that the higher the temperature of water, the faster the salt dissolved. Which graph opposite would match their results?

11 Which one of the following is **NOT** a unit of volume?

a mm

b ml

c cm^3

d l

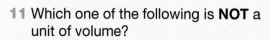

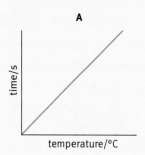

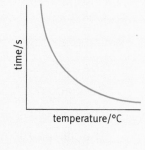

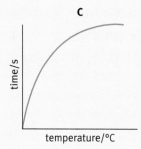

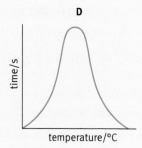

12 What is the reading on the following scale in ml?

a 41

b 40.1

c 40.5

d 42

13 Which of the following is the heaviest mass?

a 500 g

b 600 mg

c 50 kg

d 600 g

14 Which of the following distances is the shortest?

a 0.2 cm

b 2 mm

c 0.1m

d 0.1 mm

15 Which quantity is measured by a measuring cylinder?

a Mass   b Temperature   c Time   d Volume

16 Which one of the following sources of energy is a possible solution to the energy challenges faced by the Caribbean?

a Natural gas   b Crude oil   c Coal   d Solar

17 Which word means the same as 'procedure' in a scientific investigation?

a Aim   b Hypothesis   c Method   d Evaluation

Module 2 Investigating matter

1 Which one of the following substances is a liquid at 20 °C?

a Wax   b Solder   c Diesel   d Hydrogen

2 Which of the following substances is a gas at 20 °C?

a Chlorine   b Water   c Petrol   d Nitric acid

3 Which one of the following statements is true?

a The particles in a liquid have lots of space between them.

b Solids do not have a fixed or definite shape.

c The particles in a gas are always rising.

d The particles in a solid are constantly vibrating.

4 In which of the following are particles fixed in position relative to each other?

a Solid   b Liquid   c Gas   d Solution

For questions 5–8, choose from the list of options below:

a melting

b condensing

c boiling

d subliming

What terms are used for the following changes of state?

5 solid ⟶ gas

6 gas ⟶ liquid

7 liquid ⟶ gas

8 solid ⟶ liquid

9 What change of state is shown in the diagram below?

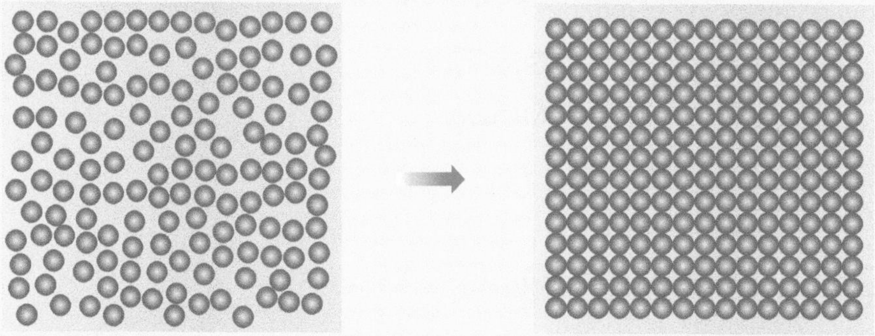

   a   evaporating   b condensing   c melting   d freezing

10 When water moves through a partially permeable membrane from a dilute solution to a concentrated solution, the process is called:

   a dissolving   b osmosis   c diffusion   d distillation

11 A mixture of insoluble chalk dust stirred up in water is called a:

   a suspension   b solution   c solvent   d solute

12 What would be the best way to separate a mixture of oil and water that has been allowed to settle?

   a Chromatography

   b Evaporation

   c Decanting

   d Simple distillation

13 Which row below shows the chemical symbols of iron and sulphur?

	Iron	Sulphur
a	I	S
b	Ir	Su
c	Fe	Su
d	Fe	S

14 A solution has a pH value of 5. What is the best description of the solution?

   a Strongly acidic   b Weakly acidic

   c Strongly alkaline   d Weakly alkaline

15 Which of the following particles are NOT found inside atoms?

 a Molecules   b Electrons

 c Protons   d Neutrons

16 Which one of the following elements is a liquid at room temperature?

 a Sulphur   b Magnesium

 c Lead   d Mercury

17 Which of the following elements is a non-metal?

 a Carbon   b Sodium

 c Aluminium   d Mercury

Module 3 Understanding life

1 Which of the following is not common to both plants and animals?

 a Respiration

 b Response to stimuli

 c Photosynthesis

 d Reproduction

2 Opposite is a diagram of an animal cell.

 Structures I, II, III refer to:

 a nucleus, cell membrane and mitochondria

 b cell membrane, mitochondria and nucleus

 c nucleus, mitochondria and cell membrane

 d mitochondria, cell membrane and nucleus

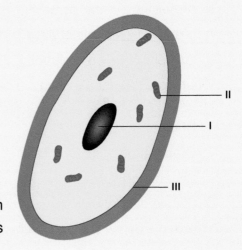

3 Which of the following is the correct order of organisation in an animal?

 a Cells – Tissues – Organs – Systems – Organism

 b Organism – Systems – Organs – Tissues – Cells

 c Tissues – Cells – Systems – Organs – Organisms

 d Systems – Organisms – Cells – Organs – Tissues

4 Which of the following statements is incorrect?

 a The nervous system coordinates responses.

 b The excretory system eliminates metabolic wastes.

 c The skeletal system provides support.

 d The respiratory system breaks down food.

5 Opposite is a diagram of a food web.

Which of the following would be the most likely outcome if the insect eating bird was removed?

a An increase in the number of snakes.

b Less damage to the cabbage and lettuce.

c An increase in the number of grasshoppers and caterpillars.

d Increase in the lizards.

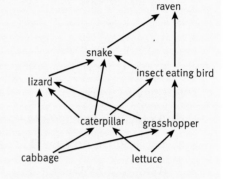

6 What is the number of chains from producer to snake in the food web?

   a 3   b 4   c 5   d 6

7 What are the raw materials in photosynthesis?

a Food and water.   b Water and carbon dioxide.

c Sunlight and oxygen.   d Chlorophyll and food.

8 What is the primary product of respiration?

a Energy   b Glucose   c Food   d CO_2

9 Which of the following is true of exhaled air?

a It contains no oxygen.

b It contains only CO_2.

c It contains more CO_2 than inhaled air.

d It contains more O_2 than inhaled air.

10 Opposite is a sketch of a flower. What are the parts labelled I and II?

a Stigma and petal

b Anther and ovary

c Stamen and stigma

d Ovary and anther

11 What part of the flower in most cases develops to form the fruit?

a The ovary   b The anther   c The petals   d The ovules

12 Which of the following is not necessary for germination?

a Air   b Water   c Light   d Suitable temperature

13 A wasp that eats caterpillars is released in a vegetable garden. This is an example of:

a Biological pest control   b Physical pest control

c Chemical pest control   d None of the above

14 A wet soil sample is sticky when rolled into a ball. What is the soil sample most likely to be?

   a A sandy soil sample

   b Suitable for most vegetable production

   c Easy to prepare

   d A clay-like soil sample

15 In a soil profile horizon D is usually:

   a rock fragments

   b dark brown due to humus content

   c parent material on rock

   d subsoil

16 What is most suitable conservation option for a vegetable garden on a steep slope?

   a Contouring   b Terracing   c Strip planting   d Ridges and furrows.

17 Nitrogen is not used in:

   a fertiliser manufacture   b food preservation

   c plant growth   d respiration

Module 4 Focusing on me

1 Which of the following is NOT generally a secondary sexual characteristic in females?

   a Widening of hips   b Pubic hair

   c Deepening of voice   d Breasts

2 The function of the testes is to:

   a produce semen   b produce the egg

   c allow for penetration   d produce the sperm

3 Which of the following are BOTH examples of barrier contraceptive methods/device?

   a Condom/sterilisation   b Diaphragm/condom

   c Sterilisation/pill   d Pill/condom

4 Pre- and post-natal care involves all of the following except:

   a immunisation   b prostate exam

   c testing for STIs   d clinic visits

5 The fusion of the male and female sex cells is called:

   a respiration   b fertilisation   c contraception   d penetration

6 Which one of the following is a nutrition-related disease?

   a Leukaemia   b Goitre   c Malaria   d Yellow fever

7 How are carbohydrates from food used in the human body?

   a To facilitates metabolism

   b For growth and repair

   c To develop muscle

   d To supply energy

8 A piece of bread is tested with a few drops of iodine solution. The iodine solution will turn:

   a red/brown   b violet   c red   d blue/black

9 A food shows a positive protein test with Biuret solution. The solution will turn:

   a red/brown   b violet   c red   d blue/black

Questions **10–13** refer to the following four options:

   a Red blood cells

   b White blood cells

   c Platelets

   d Plasma

10 Which component in blood carries oxygen around the body?

11 Which component in blood helps it to clot at the site of a cut in the skin?

12 Which component in blood is a straw coloured liquid that transports dissolved substances?

13 Which component in blood protects you against infectious diseases?

14 Which one of the following is **NOT** a blood group?

   a A   b O   c AA   d AB

15 Which part of the circulatory system is described below?

They have a large lumen, thin walls and valves which prevent the back-flow of blood.

   a Arteries   b Veins   c Capillaries   d Atria

Module 5 Exploring energy

1 Which form of energy is stored in food?

   a Electrical   b Light   c Chemical   d Heat

2 A box standing on a high shelf has which form of energy?

   a Solar   b Sound   c Kinetic   d Potential

3 Which of these statements is true?

   a Energy is neither created nor destroyed, but is changed from one form to another.

   b Energy can be created, but not destroyed and cannot be changed from one form to another.

   c Energy is neither created nor destroyed and cannot be changed from one form to another.

   d Energy cannot be created, but can be destroyed and changed from one form to another.

4 Which one of the energy sources below is renewable?

   a Geothermal   b Oil   c Natural gas   d Coal

5 Which one of the following is a disadvantage of generating electricity using wind power?

   a It produces gases that pollute the atmosphere.

   b It produces solid waste that pollutes land, rivers and lakes.

   c It uses up the Earth's limited resources.

   d It takes up a lot of space to build a wind farm.

6 Which one of these gases is released when a fossil fuel burns in large amounts of air?

   a Carbon dioxide   b Hydrogen

   c Carbon monoxide   d Nitrogen

7 Which one of the following is the best explanation of how a fossil fuel was formed?

   a Black rock buried deep underground, was compressed and decomposed, and converted into a fossil fuel.

   b The remains of animals and plants that lived millions of years ago were buried, compressed and heated to form fossil fuels.

   c Animal droppings were preserved as fossils which can now be dug up and used directly as fossil fuels.

   d The gases given off from the waste of farm animals can be used directly as a fossil fuel.

8 Which one of the following is an electrical conductor?

   a Plastic   b Brass   c Wood   d Glass

9 Electrical cables are covered in a layer of plastic to:

   a warn users of the danger of electricity

   b make the cable more flexible

   c protect the user from electrocution

   d prevent the wastage of electrical energy

10 What is the symbol used for the unit of electrical power?

   a J   b A

   c V   d W

11 Which one of the electrical circuits opposite is a parallel circuit?

12 Here are the electricity meter readings from a house at the start and end of a week. How much electrical energy was used in the week?

13 If electrical energy costs 57 cents per unit, how much does the electrical energy used in the week cost?

14 Which one of the following materials is magnetic?

   a Aluminium   b Plastic

   c Wax   d Steel

15 Which of the following shows the magnetic field around a bar magnet?

16 We often get a sea breeze on the coast. Which process causes the sea breeze on a sunny day?

   a Convection

   b Conduction

   c Radiation

   d Reflection

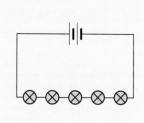

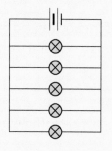

10,000   1,000   100   10   1

Monday

10,000   1,000   100   10   1

Saturday

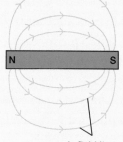

magnetic field lines

A

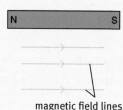

magnetic field lines

B

Glossary

air resistance: the force of friction caused by movement of an object through air

antibodies: proteins made as a reaction to antigens on foreign materials in the body, such as bacteria

antigens: a harmful substance which enters the body and causes the body to make antibodies as a response to fight off disease

balanced diet: meals that provide sufficient quantities of each essential food group

carnivore: a meat-eater

carpel: the female part of a flower; it consists of the stigma, style and ovary

cell membrane: the outer layer of the cell; it lets simple substances pass into or out of the cell

cell walls: surround the cell contents (together with their cell membrane) with a rigid boundary; this gives the cell support and shape

chloroplasts: the green structures in plant cells where photosynthesis takes place; photosynthesis is the process by which plants make food

compress: to squash

concentration: this is a measure of how much of a substance is present in a given volume of a mixture; for example, it can be expressed in grams per litre (or g/l) of the mixture

conduction: the transfer of heat energy from an energy source through a substance

consumer: an organism that eats another organism lower down the food chain

contraception: methods used to prevent a woman from getting pregnant

control variables: the things you need to keep the same in each test to make your investigation a fair test

convection: the transfer of energy through fluids (liquids and gases)

cytoplasm: the jelly-like liquid inside the cell; most of the chemical reactions needed to keep us alive happen in this solution; for example, our cells get the energy they need from respiration, which takes place here

deficiency disease: illness caused by a lack of certain vitamins or minerals

dependent variable: the thing you measure to judge the effect of changing the independent variable

ductile: can be drawn out into wire

embryo: an animal in the initial stages of growth following fertlisation

evaporation: the changing of a liquid to a gas

fertilisation: when sex cells, for example a sperm and an egg, or a pollen grain nucleus and an ovule nucleus, join together to make a new individual

fertiliser: a substance that provides one or more essential nutrients for healthy plant growth

filtration: the mixture of a solid and liquid is poured through filter paper – a special type of paper with tiny holes which cannot be seen with the naked eye; the water molecules pass through the holes, but those in the insoluble solid do not because they are too big

food chain: a sequence of organisms with each successive organism eating the one before it

food web: the inter-connection of food chains in an ecosystem

fossil fuels: non-renewable fuels made from the remains of plants or tiny sea creatures that lived millions of years ago; for example coal, crude oil and natural gas

germination: the start of the growth of a seed

herbivore: a plant-eater

hypothesis: a scientific idea suggested in order to explain a prediction or data

immunised: when a person's immune system is strengthened against a particular disease or diseases; a vaccine is given to the patient via an injection of orally

independent variable: the thing you decide to change in each test in your investigation

lustrous: shiny

malleable: can be hammered into shapes without breaking into smaller pieces

mitochondria (sg. mitochondrion): found in the cytoplasm; they are the sites where respiration takes place and energy is released from our food; they are the energy factories of the cell

newton (N): the unit of force

nucleus: the 'control centre' of the cell; it controls all the activities in the cell

organ system: a group of organs that perform one of the vital aspects of life in an organism

organ: a collection of tissues that perform a particular function as part of one of the organ systems in a living thing

ova: egg cells in animals

ovaries: the parts of the female reproductive system which release eggs and produce hormones or the part of a flower which makes ovules

ovule: egg cells in plants

pesticide: a chemical used to destroy insects or animals that damage crops

platelets: fragments of cells used in blood clotting

pollination: the transfer of a plant's male sex cells to a female part of a plant before fertilisation can take place

producer: green plants that make their own food by photosynthesis

puberty: the time when the development of the sex organs is completed

radiation: the heat energy given off from hot objects.

respiration: the process in which cells use glucose to release the energy needed

semen: a mixture of sperm and liquid for the sperm to move in

soil erosion: the wearing away and removal of soil from its original location by the action of wind or water

sonorous: makes a ringing sound when struck with a hard object

stamen: the male part of a flower; it consists of the anther and filament

states of matter: solid, liquid or gas

testes: part of the male reproductive system in which sperm is made

tissues: groups of cells of the same type which work together to carry out a particular function

toxic: poisonous

universal donor: a person with blood group O who can donate blood to another person of any blood group

universal recipient: a person with blood group AB who can receive blood donated by another person of any blood group

vaccinated: see 'immunised'

vacuole: the large central part of the plant cell which is full of cell sap (liquid); this helps to support the plant structure and to store substances

weight: the force of gravity acting on an object, measured in newtons (N)

Index